B

D0220758

Emma Goldman

American Individualist

Emma Goldman
1869–1940

Emma Goldman

American Individualist

John Chalberg

Edited by Oscar Handlin

HarperCollins*Publishers*

Sponsoring Editor: Bruce D. Borland
Project Coordination: Chernow Editorial Services, Inc.
Text Design: Heidi Fieschko
Cover Art: The Art Comp.
Frontispiece photo: The Schlesinger Library, Radcliffe College
Photo Research: Ferret Research, Inc.
Compositor: Pam Frye Typesetting, Inc.
Printer and Binder: Malloy Lithographing, Inc.

EMMA GOLDMAN

Copyright © 1991 by John Chalberg

All rights reserved. Printed in the United States of America. No part of this
book may be used or reproduced in any manner whatsoever without written
permission, except in the case of brief quotations embodied in critical articles
and reviews. For information address HarperCollins Publishers Inc., 10 East
53rd Street, New York, NY 10022.

Library of Congress Cataloging in Publication Data

Chalberg, John.
    Emma Goldman : American individualist / John Chalberg ; edited by
Oscar Handlin.
        p.   cm. — (The Library of American biography)
    Includes bibliographical references and index.
    ISBN 0-673-52102-8
    1. Goldman, Emma, 1869–1940. 2. Anarchists—United States—
Biography.   I. Handlin, Oscar, 1915. II. Title. III. Series.
HX843.7.G65C48   1991
335'.83'092—dc20
    [B]   90-20170
                                                                        CIP

91 92 93 94 9 8 7 6 5 4 3 2 1

Contents

Editor's Preface

From early youth, Emma Goldman lived in rebellion, impatiently shaking off every restraint. She resented her parents, left her family, migrated to America, moved restlessly from one lover to another—never finding fulfillment. Deeply interested in politics and in improving the welfare of the laboring masses, she nevertheless accepted the discipline of no party, nor even of any coherent ideology. Nor did she take gracefully to limitations imposed by gender in nineteenth-century America. Always she put herself at the center of her universe, seeking fulfillment as a person—in that sense a romantic heroine. In one setting after another she discovered that a hard, unyielding world doomed her efforts to defeat.

Yet in the very process of unending struggle, her life threw light on the context of the society through which she moved. The East European setting she put behind her as a young girl when she sailed off to the New World, and the life of the impoverished immigrants among whom she lived in the United States, formed the background of her experiences. In the very process by which she strove to change or put them behind her she exposed the harsh conditions against which she rebelled.

Her career also revealed a great deal about the texture of American radicalism at the end of the nineteenth century. In Britain, France, and Germany, rigid lines marked off various critics of the industrial society that emerged between 1880 and 1910. In the United States the intellectual situation was much more fluid. Scores of autonomous critics launched their attacks on the brutalities of the wage system and on the hardships of slum life. Among them were followers of Henry George and Edward Bellamy, or Karl Marx and Peter Kropotkin, socialists, anarchists, and reformers devoted to one cause or another. Emma considered herself an anarchist for many years but did not establish a formal party affiliation. Nor was she patient with

the subtleties of socialism. Indeed, she accepted no party platform. She spoke out on issues that concerned women, not only
suffrage and temperance but also sexuality, birth control, and
the family. Above all she hated war and threw herself into the
struggle for peace.

Professor Chalberg's thoughtful account of this passionate character throws light on her personal qualities, and also
on the whole social background against which she led her life,
in the unending struggle to realize herself by improving the
conditions of others.

Oscar Handlin

Author's Preface

When I first envisioned writing a biography of Emma Goldman for this series I was convinced that my subject had as much to say to late 20th-century Americans as she did to Americans of her day. That was two long years ago. Little did I then realize just how right I would turn out to be. In the interim, Communism has collapsed, the Cold War appears to be drawing to a close, and the virtues of the market tumble from strange sets of lips.

Well, nearly seventy years ago Emma Goldman gave the world a firsthand glimpse of the failures and horrors of Communism. Eighty, ninety, and one hundred years ago she also gave Americans fits over her personal indictment of the failures and horrors of capitalism.

Goldman was always a thorn in the side of her enemies, not to mention her friends and complete strangers. Perhaps it is only fitting that she play a similar role from the grave. In any event, her criticisms of everything from corporate capitalism, to timid reformers, to modern feminism, to marriage and family life, to all brands of totalitarianism, and to all forms of democracy reveal her to be a woman for many more seasons than could be contained in her seventy years, roughly half of which she spent in the United States.

That Goldman still speaks to American audiences will, I hope, soon become apparent to you. That she seldom offers reassurance and comfort will also, I trust, be evident. As a white male, a native Minnesotan (where niceness reigns supreme), a reticent Scandinavian, a husband and father of more children than the national average, and a suburbanite with the inevitable two-car garage and obligatory mortgage, I can testify that living with Goldman has not been reassuring or comforting. But it has been interesting.

Now for the much deserved acknowledgments—minus my innate reticence. Good editors are as scarce as good anarchists in the streets of Bloomington, Minnesota. I have been fortunate to stumble on more than my share. A former student, Pat Lassonde, read more chapters more times that she originally anticipated. Thank goodness she did. An experienced editor and a trained historian, she whipped both my prose and my ideas into much better shape than I had thought possible. An unreformed newspaperwoman and Normandale Commmunity College colleague, Jo Ann Rice, read more than one version of many chapters, focused her skilled eye on paragraphs that were not exactly bursting with vitality, and reminded me that good writing and good history are not necessarily incompatible. Sue Cyphers, who serves as faculty secretary for many more people than is consistent with maintaining one's mental health, interrupted her work all too frequently—and always cheerfully—to help me master the intricacies of word processing.

Friends and fellow historians Tom Jones of Metropolitan State University and Kevin Byrne of Gustavus Adolphus College remain friends—despite their trenchant (and valued) criticism along the way. They encouraged me when I needed encouragement and deflated me when I didn't think I needed deflating. They were always honest in their evaluations of my work. After all, what are friends for, if not to be used—and honest?

Finally, I wish to thank Professor Oscar Handlin for placing his confidence in an unknown quantity from a Midwestern community college far removed from both his world and Goldman's. His editorial skills left me alternately amazed (how did he lead me from there to here without missing a beat or a verb?) and chagrined (how could I have written such an awful passage in the first place?). That this book exists at all, I owe to him.

In a very real sense, this book also owes its existence to my late father, John E. Chalberg, dean and later president of Brainerd Junior College, who, by his example, taught me the value of education, the importance of fairness, and the benefits of kindness; and to Professor Gordon Ross, once of Regis College, who taught me a good deal of history, inspired me to learn more, and almost deterred me from a disastrous (and thankfully brief) detour through law school.

No one in my immediate family served in any formal editorial capacity. All of them figured, I suppose, that they had listened to enough of Goldman's story to excuse them from having to read it as well. All were supportive nonetheless. Besides listening patiently, my wife Janet occasionally reminded me that I had family obligations of a nuclear variety, even if Goldman did not. Besides listening dutifully, my mother, Mildred O'Brien Chalberg, has always been a great reader and my best audience. And never has she been the kind of mother Goldman warned the world against. Besides listening bemusedly, daughters Kristin and Sarah tolerated their father's fascination with something so unfashionable as history. Between cries and shrieks, young sons Michael and Stephen did their best to keep family life in a state of anarchy not at all in accord with Goldman's fondest dreams. Besides, every one of them thinks that whatever I write is just fine.

Since extensive community college teaching duties and writing books are not necessarily complementary, I thought I ought to dedicate this volume to a number of individuals while I have a chance – namely to the women in my life. I have lived with each of them longer than I have lived with Goldman. Each has done her share to make life at least as interesting as life with the real Goldman might have been. Beyond that a reticent Midwestern Scandinavian male should not – and will not – go.

John Chalberg

CHAPTER ONE

Prologue

Border crossings between the United States and Canada today are generally routine affairs. Not so a midwinter trek of a single woman from the Canadian to the American side of Niagara Falls several decades ago. A reporter on the scene described the woman as a "grandmotherly person with a blue twinkling eye." The host customs officer dutifully recorded the rest: "age, 64; height, five feet one-half inch; eyes, blue; hair, blond-gray; face, round." He might have added "disposition, buoyant," had he only been aware of her persistently depressed frame of mind over the preceding months.

It was February 1934, and Emma Goldman had finally come home. For the first time in better than fourteen years the once notorious Red Emma stood on American soil. For the first time since her deportation from the United States, she could look forward to traveling and speaking from New York City to points west. For the first time since the Red Scare of 1919, she was in her element.

The Emma Goldman of 1934 was not the Emma Goldman of 1919, but she was still anxious to be heard and still able to stir emotions. A grandmotherly Red Emma may have lost some of her spell, more of her confidence, and most of her following, but she remained capable of hurling out words full of bite and wit in response to her critics and in defense of anarchism.

Anarchism had been Goldman's governing philosophy for virtually all of her thirty-four years in the United States. For all that time—and longer—the word itself had been loaded with meanings for both anarchists and their enemies. It derives from two Greek words, *arche,* meaning "power" or "violence," and *an,* meaning "without." The word, therefore, implies a rejection of all authority. But to Goldman anarchists were not mere naysayers. Nor were they random bomb throwers or indiscriminate free lovers. Anarchy, to this anarchist, was not chaos but a way of living grounded in voluntarism. Anarchists of her persuasion and generation did not spurn order, they simply objected to enforced order, whether the enforcer was the state, a monarch, a president, a legislature, a court, a husband, or a parent. Anarchists wanted to eliminate all external authorities so that all people would be free to pursue interests—whether individual or communal—of their own choosing.

Anarchism, as defined by Goldman, was the "philosophy of a new social order based on liberty unrestricted by man-made law." It was the "theory that all forms of government rest on violence and are therefore wrong and harmful, as well as unnecessary." To her, anarchism was the "only philosophy which brings to man the consciousness of himself; which maintains that God, the State, and society are nonexistent."

The Emma Goldman of 1919 had made a career of challenging the legitimacy of religion, government, and property. She was prepared to pursue her public and private war against this triad when the U.S. government moved to bring her down. Long a target of the Justice Department for her outspoken advocacy of anarchism, she was deported from the United States in December for a variety of reasons. Officially, anarchists had been persona non grata since 1903 and the passage of the Anarchist Exclusion Act. Specifically, she had angered a series of U.S. governments by supporting workers' causes, endorsing birth control, embracing purveyors of violence, and opposing both American entry into World War I and the drafting of soldiers for duty in Europe. Finally, the Justice Department of Attorney General A. Mitchell Palmer and a young underling named J. Edgar Hoover determined that she was not a U.S. citizen, thereby making her eligible to receive her unwanted eviction notice.

Nonetheless, Goldman was quite prepared to go. Her new home was to be her old home—Mother Russia. Having left czarist Russia for America thirty-four years earlier, Goldman expected to see anarchism flourish in Soviet Russia. Instead, she discovered that Lenin's Russia was far from being an anarchist's paradise. In fact, Lenin had much less tolerance for anarchist dissenters than did the redoubtable Hoover. Her dreams and expectations shattered, Goldman took leave of the Soviet Union in 1921 to live the uncertain life of a European nomad.

From her vantage point in Europe, Goldman saw few signs of a resurgent anarchism anywhere in the world through the 1920s and early 1930s. An optimist by nature, she also knew when she had to face reality—even when that reality did little to relieve an enveloping sense of gloom that seemed to dominate so much of her life in exile.

Despite her bouts with depression, Goldman continued to tour and to talk, albeit with dwindling energy and fading hope. By the spring of 1933 she would write her long-time compatriot and one-time lover, Alexander Berkman, that she was "tired of chasing windmills." Yet, in that very same letter she could revert to her role as cheerleader for her movement: "We must go on in our work. We are voices in the wilderness, much more so now than forty years ago. I mean voices for liberty. No one wants it anymore. Yet it seems to me that just because of the present mad clamor for dictatorship, we of all people should not give up. Someday, sometime long after we are gone, liberty may again raise its proud head. It is up to us to blaze its way—dim as our torch may seem today—it is still the one flame."

In this letter, Goldman was hurt by the refusal of the masses to listen to her and angered by their apparent "mad clamor for dictatorship." Still, she knew no other life and no other message. Abandonment of her ideal (anarchism) was out of the question. If the "wilderness" had grown more dense, the more reason she had to shout louder and longer.

Still, Goldman's world was closing in on her, and no one knew this better than she. Gone were her days of ecstasy and optimism. Gone were the days when she could draw and move a crowd. Gone were the days when she truly believed that the workers of the world could be transformed into living and breathing, working and playing anarchists.

Instead, Goldman thought that the workers of an economically depressed Western world "hugged their chains." The "deeper" those chains bit "into their flesh," the more the workers seemed to "admire their masters." To Goldman, therefore, the enemy was not just a Hitler or a Stalin, a Woodrow Wilson or an A. Mitchell Palmer. The enemy was everywhere and virtually everybody. Her new enemies, she feared, were the anonymous workers who had once been her potential friends and allies, who had once gathered around her as she hurled forth her message from New York to San Diego and countless points in between.

It was too late for Goldman to stop, even if it was also too soon for her to claim victory. Maybe she could recapture a piece of her past, a bit of her magic, if only she could undertake one final American lecture tour. Even at sixty-four and long absent from the United States, Goldman continued to believe, however faintly, that in the United States she would once again find her true audience. Perhaps only in the land of eternal optimism would she be able to restore her own flagging faith in the future and regain a measure of confidence in herself and in her cause.

What delicious irony! In 1919 an angry Emma Goldman had literally thumbed her nose at an America that had first spurned her. In 1934 an expectant Emma Goldman anticipated a new day in the land of second chances. But was anarchism a realistic alternative for the United States of Franklin Roosevelt? In truth, anarchism was almost irrelevant at a time when the Great Depression was prompting schemes for expanding, not retracting, government at all levels.

Goldman never liked to think of herself as irrelevant. Nor did she enjoy her years in exile. Hence, she decided to orchestrate her own return. Unlike Berkman, she could never bring herself simply to hate America. In fact, she had long considered herself to be an American—even if any number of American presidents, congressmen, bureaucrats, and policemen had disagreed with her. Enemies Goldman had aplenty, but she also had friends in the United States, even influential friends, and she was not embarrassed to use them to get what she wanted. Roger Baldwin of the American Civil Liberties Union, writers Sinclair Lewis and Sherwood Anderson, critic H. L. Mencken, and philosopher John Dewey were all members of a Goldman inspired committee to bring Goldman back to America, back to the country where she thought she belonged.

Goldman even had friends and admirers in the Roosevelt administration. New Deal agencies were honeycombed with old progressives, many of whom had known or had at least known of Goldman. Besides, this was the eve of the Popular Front, which called for liberals, communists, socialists, and, yes, even anarchists to band together against the greater enemy—fascism. "No enemies to the left" would soon be their rallying cry. The Roosevelt administration's diplomatic recognition of the Soviet Union at the end of 1933 was a harbinger of a new day. (In fact, the exchange of ambassadors between Washington and Moscow was set to take place that very February of 1934.)

Diplomatic negotiations between the Department of Labor and Goldman were almost as complex. Labor Secretary Frances Perkins insisted that Goldman agree in advance of her visit not to lecture on political affairs, only on literary topics. Goldman contended that "every creative expression must have its being in the social and political fabric of the time." In between was Roger Baldwin, who urged Goldman to go along with Perkins's proviso as a "sporting proposition." To Baldwin, the dispute was meaningless: once in the country Goldman could advance her own theories of "literary criticism." In the end, she agreed, thereby clearing the way for her to return to the United States at long last.

The Emma Goldman of 1919 would not have submitted to the whims of a government official, even if that official happened to be a woman and a feminist. Cooperating with the powerful was a game that Goldman had never sought to master. Now, at least, she had to play it. Coming home, even for her allotted ninety days, was that important to her.

The years of exile had taken their toll on Goldman. After souring on the Bolshevik revolution, she had become an anarchist without roots, a woman without a country—even though she had tried living in quite a few. By definition, of course, an anarchist should take pride in a lack of connections. But not Goldman in exile.

The story of Goldman's final three months in the United States was not a happy one. Hers was not a triumphal tour. Neither her morale nor her movement was revived by her presence. Still, from 1934 until her death in 1940, Goldman's self-appointed mission was to keep the spirit of anarchism alive. Given her history, no one was better poised than she to hover over what remained of the worldwide anarchist movement.

Goldman in or out of exile might have claimed to be an anarchist first, but she was actually an American first, an anarchist second, and a very American anarchist always. For the better part of thirty-four years, this Jewish immigrant lived, loved, and fought on American soil. During these years she suffered her share of defeats, political and otherwise; but from her memory of these years she savored her moments of ecstasy, political and otherwise.

Yes, Goldman could be ambivalent about the United States. Among her many affairs she carried on a perpetual love-hate relationship with America. Lecturing in Toronto in 1926, she found herself tantalizingly close to the United States. "Loving America as a woman loves a man," she wanted desperately to board a train for Detroit, if only to "help make America ridiculous again." But by 1934 ambivalence had given way to a conviction that she knew where she belonged—and wanted to be. By then she had come to realize when she had been her happiest. America's founding document bestows on its citizens the right to pursue happiness. Few who lived in America were in hotter pursuit than was one of its official noncitizens.

The American dream was Goldman's dream just as much as it was that of Andrew Carnegie or Woodrow Wilson or anyone else who felt the sting of her wrath. In fact, the American dream has always been many dreams. Some people dream of acquiring great wealth; others dream of little more than a home to call their own. Some seek to wield great power and achieve great notoriety; others seek to lead peaceful and anonymous lives. Goldman's American dream focused on achieving equality and individuality for all—and on possessing power and fame for herself. She needed to dominate others—her friends as well as her enemies—and craved celebrity. And she reveled in notoriety.

The story of her years in the United States is the story of the Americanization of Goldman, not because she doggedly climbed the social ladder, but because of her desire to be the center of attention, to be someone who mattered, to be known. At some point the messenger (Goldman) became more important than the message (anarchism). At about the same point, Goldman's version of anarchism became, for her, inextricably linked to the American reform tradition.

By the time of her deportation, Goldman was an individualist first and a revolutionary second. Although never reluctant to call herself an anarchist, she was increasingly anxious to establish herself as a direct intellectual descendant of Thomas Jefferson and Tom Paine and Henry David Thoreau. She knew that the America of 1919 was not the America of 1776, but she did insist that her enemies were the inevitable enemies of anyone willing to challenge the status quo or live apart from the mass of men and women: the state, whether monarchical or democratic; aristocrats, whether titled or moneyed; and ignorance in all its forms.

Goldman's life should not conjure up for readers visions of a Garden of Eden for Jeffersonian yeoman farmers. Her America was an urban America, an immigrants' America, a woman's America. Her ideal America was also filled with independent individuals, whether they were first-generation Jewish immigrants, fourth-generation female office workers, seventh-generation wives and mothers, husbands and fathers, sons and daughters, or even first-generation single women.

Repression, whether economic, political, or psychological, was Goldman's perpetual enemy. In combating it, she quickly learned to employ the uniquely American vocabulary of individualism. She may not have been exactly what Jefferson had in mind when he preached the virtues of American individualism, but she was determined to act out the American fascination with personal freedom—and to act for wives victimized by their husbands, factory workers under the thumb of foremen, and World War I draftees anxious to escape the steely gaze of Uncle Sam.

In a sense, Goldman herself was always on the run, if not from the government of Uncle Sam, then from any confinement. Her commitment was to herself and to her definition of anarchism. She refused to make other commitments. Ambivalence, not commitment, was her governing principle for much of her adult life. Personal autonomy freed her from the entreaties of lovers and the burdens of children, as well as from the demands of other radicals and the agenda of contemporary feminists. Love and romance were important, but permanent relationships were always difficult. That absence of permanence also characterized Goldman's approach to labor unionists, Wobblies (members of the Industrial Workers of the World, the militant labor organization founded in 1905), socialists, pacifists, birth control advocates, and suffragists. All were occasional allies, but none could provide Goldman with an enduring home or a fixed reference point. No one, not even her beloved "Sasha" (Berkman), ever served as her constant comrade.

Goldman's willingness to live apart from the herd, her commitment to uncommitment, had its drawbacks, chief among them a life filled with more than its share of emptiness, of unrequested solitude away from the next podium after yet another rally. She tried her best to keep those idle moments to a minimum. She also refused to choose between her public and her private lives. It was her way of remaining uncommitted and of filling the inevitable void at the same time.

Still, Goldman had opportunities for introspection—both before and after her 1919 deportation. There was time, therefore, for Goldman to know herself. In one sense she knew herself very well indeed. She realized that she was a public person who relished the attention she received. She was also aware of discrepancies between her public persona and her private self. In the middle of her most public years, she wrote to Ben Reitman, the single greatest love of her life: "If ever our correspondence should be published, the world would stand aghast that I, Emma Goldman, the strong revolutionist, the daredevil, the one who has defied laws and convention, should have been as helpless [in love] as a shipwrecked crew on a foaming ocean."

Was the essential Emma Goldman the helpless lover or the ardent revolutionary? Or was she the ardent lover and the ineffectual revolutionary? In truth, she was all of the above at various points in her turbulent life. In her autobiography, *Living My Life,* Goldman recounted an exchange with a New York artist-anarchist anxious to get the "real Emma Goldman" on canvas. Goldman hesitated. She was busy. Others had tried to capture her without success. Besides, she wondered, "Which is the real one?" Try as she might, she had "never been able to unearth her."

Despite her objections, Goldman sat and the artist worked. The result was a portrait that her sister Helena later saw on exhibition in Rochester. "I should not have known it was you if your name had not been under it." True to form, Goldman never bothered to view the painting. Looking for the real Emma Goldman was not a high priority, satisfied as she was to live her life rather than examine it.

Who, then, was the real Emma Goldman? She was an American, if never officially an American citizen. Much of her individualism was American. Many of her heroes and heroines turned out to be American. Even her anarchism was American in the way she advertised herself and lived her life.

During the 1960s there was an Emma Goldman revival among American dissidents. A new generation of feminists found her mettle, if not her anarchism, admirable. Another army of antiwar protesters drew sustenance from her unforgiving opposition to World War I. And counterculturists came to realize that their version of bohemianism was not the first to thumb its collective nose at conventional America. In sum, challengers to both the political and cultural status quo discovered a long ago ally in Emma Goldman.

During that same decade some defenders of that status quo took to sporting bumper stickers that read: "America: Love It Or Leave It." Given Goldman's open war against American orthodoxy and its enforcers, she would have understood the sentiment. But, given a choice, she would not have acted on the command. America was her home, too.

CHAPTER TWO

Arrivals

"Herded together like cattle," a young girl and her older sister battled terror and seasickness aboard the steamer *Elbe* bound for New York City. The Atlantic passage was never comfortable for 19th-century immigrants headed for the Promised Land. But traveling steerage in December assured a unique test of will and stomach for all passengers—even for the younger of these two sisters, who had left St. Petersburg without regrets.

The year was 1885. The great migration of Eastern European Jews to America had begun a few years earlier and would continue for forty years, ending only when the U.S. government acted decisively to halt the flow. In 1885 the migration was in its infancy, and these two young migrants were filled with expectations of a better future. Family awaited them in Rochester, New York, where another sister and her husband had settled a few years earlier.

For the youngest of the three sisters, a desire for freedom from home propelled her away from her past as strongly as any attraction that a free America held for her. A domineering father and a tyrannical government had convinced her that life in St. Petersburg was unbearable. Her father sought to extend his control to the point of refusing to give his consent to her emigration. Angered by his stand, she was reduced to pleading, begging, and weeping. Nothing worked. Not until she threatened to jump into the Neva River did the "old man" finally yield.

The "old man" was Abraham Goldman; his headstrong daughter was named Emma. Born on June 27, 1869, in the ancient city of Kovno (Kaunas in modern Lithuania), Emma Goldman lived all of her first sixteen years under the joint rule of her father and the czars. For most of the Jews of Kovno, czarist control dictated a life of bare subsistence within the city's Jewish ghetto. Official Russia had little interest in improving the lot of its Jewish subjects and no interest in assimilating them. Jews were confined to urban places and denied agrarian lives. Yet they did serve a purpose: They provided the larger Russian culture with an almost endless supply of scapegoats.

Ironically, Goldman herself acted out the role of scapegoat within her own family. She was the unwanted child of a father who had dreamed of having a son and of a mother whose nightmare was another child. When Abraham and Taube Goldman married in the summer of 1868, his expectations were high, hers nonexistent. At the time, Taube Zodokoff, daughter of a well-to-do doctor, was a widow with two daughters (Helena, who would travel to America with Emma, and Lena, with whom the girls intended to live once they arrived in Rochester). She did not want a third daughter—before or after her second marriage.

Abraham immediately began to squander his wife's small inheritance, thereby assuring that the ill-conceived union, which had been arranged at his request, would only grow more strained as time passed. In other circumstances and to another couple, the birth of a healthy baby girl within a year of their marriage would have been a welcome event. Not so the birth of Emma Goldman in 1869.

Even the subsequent arrival of two sons did not lift the spirits of their parents or convince the father to forgive Emma for being a girl. Spurned by his wife, Goldman rejected his daughter. To make matters worse, he went on to fail at a series of minor business ventures. The marriage survived all of this, but in name only. Nothing seemed to make Abraham or

Taube happy. Separately, they retreated to their private worlds of depression and self-pity, which they left only to do battle with one another.

Emma could not help but be aware of the tension within the household. Nor could she avoid being the target of her father's violent temper—or wishing that she might be the recipient of a mother's caressing love. As a result, she grew up in an atmosphere of great insecurity. This young girl, who would one day champion victims of oppression, was herself a victim of her parents' loveless marriage, of her father's tyranny, and of her mother's withdrawal. Abraham Goldman demanded total obedience from all of his children. For them, Emma later recalled, he generated "an atmosphere charged with antagonism and harshness." For Emma specifically he reserved the whip, for she proved to be the most willful and disobedient of the children. Nothing, however, could blunt her rebelliousness.

Taube, too, turned to violence to control her youngest daughter. She slapped Emma when she masturbated and when she menstruated for the first time (this being an old-fashioned remedy that was supposed to ward off disgrace). Within the family, only her half-sister Helena gave Emma the love she craved. But Helena, who herself was treated as little more than a servant, could not compensate for their parents' failings. As early as the age of six, Emma could recall escapades with a family servant named Petrushka. Together they idled away the afternoons when he should have been tending the family's cattle and sheep. He entertained her with his lute. She, in turn, reveled in her freedom from her chores and from her father's whip.

At the end of these rendezvous, Petrushka would carry Goldman home on his shoulders. Somewhere along the way he would suddenly stop, throw her into the air, catch her, and press her to him. Much later she would associate her first erotic sensations with these games of "horse." At the very least, the joy that she experienced with Petrushka gave Goldman a glimpse of a world where rules, whether parental or governmental, did not exist. That world came to a crushing end when her father suddenly dismissed Petrushka.

Goldman's loss, however, was only half the story. The other half was her new awareness of her father's arbitrary power over his servants. Abraham Goldman was then an innkeeper in the small Lithuanian town of Papile, where Jews were in the majority, but where German culture predominated and the czars ruled. There Goldman observed—and felt—not only her father's power, but also the power of others. A good portion of her father's livelihood depended on the renewal of his contract to manage the government-subsidized stagecoach, which the townspeople could withdraw or extend. It did not take long for the young Goldman to realize that the whims of the community had a direct impact on her father's mood and pocketbook, which in turn affected her life and the lives of the family servants.

Edicts from Moscow affected many more than Abraham Goldman's extended family. His inn also served as a military induction center for the czar. At regular intervals a wide-eyed Goldman witnessed both the power of the state and the anguish of mothers (her own included) when sons were taken away.

Formal education did not soften Goldman's attitude toward either the government or her own family. At the age of seven she was sent to the Prussian seaport of Königsberg (now Kaliningrad) to live with relatives and attend a private Jewish elementary school. There she found life even harsher and more restrictive than under her father's roof. She was forced to share a bed with an aunt and work as a servant to a bully of an uncle. In short order, the uncle decided that education was a waste of time for a young girl and promptly removed Goldman from the school. She instantly protested, only to have her uncle join the growing list of adults who used violence on her. On this occasion Goldman was actually rescued by her father, who, she later remembered, embraced her for the first time in years.

Shortly thereafter Abraham Goldman moved the entire family to Königsberg, and the young Goldman again enrolled in school, this time in a public school, where beatings were everyday occurrences. Despite her father's misgivings about the benefits of an educated daughter, Goldman remained in the same school for six years, during which time she learned more from her rebellions against sadistic teachers than she did from her books.

Only a young teacher of German befriended Goldman by inviting her into her home and introducing her to opera and literature. The teacher also took seriously the girl's desire to become a doctor, a desire that served only to add to her mounting frustrations. With her teacher's encouragement, Goldman passed her entrance examinations for her next level of schooling only to be denied the required letter of good character by another teacher, who declared her to be a "terrible child [who] would grow into a worse woman."

But in 1881, twelve-year-old Emma Goldman was not yet prepared to abandon her dream of further education. When her father accepted a business position in a cousin's dry goods establishment in St. Petersburg, she looked forward to a new and better school. Life with her family was still horrid, but at least St. Petersburg was a large city with many schools. She knew that school was still her best avenue of escape.

A capital city of architectural grandeur, artistic beauty, and private wealth, St. Petersburg contained a significant Jewish community of some 17,000 people. Living in this city were some of the wealthiest Jews in all of Russia. Abraham Goldman was not among them. In fact, his family was closer to the bottom than to the top of the social pyramid—and headed decisively in the wrong direction.

The dry goods shop collapsed even before the family arrived to join their father. Money for daily living expenses, as well as for Abraham's next venture (a small grocery store), had to be borrowed from Taube's brothers. Meanwhile, the three sisters all had to work. For Goldman, that meant everything from knitting shawls at home to outside employment first in a glove factory and then in a corset shop. Formal schooling was completely out of the question. Informally, however, she began to obtain a St. Petersburg education, which "changed my very being and the whole course of my life."

Between her departure from Königsberg and her arrival in America four years later, Goldman inadvertently prepared herself for her subsequent plunge into radical politics. Economic hardship was immediate and pressing. But for her that hardship—and the lowly jobs she obtained in order to combat it—was only a small part of her story. More significant were her ongoing battles with her father and a single encounter with an anonymous hotel clerk. At the heart of both stories were sexual dilemmas that Goldman was never really able to resolve.

As Goldman neared the age of fifteen, her father determined that it was time for her to marry. Having arbitrarily concluded that she was a "loose" girl, he regarded marriage as the sole alternative. Besides, it was time that someone else took care of her. The girl begged to be permitted to continue her studies, insisting that she would never marry for any reason but love. At the time of her successful threat to leap into the Neva, there had been no marriage—and no resolution of the argument.

As it happened, Goldman was fifteen when she had her first overtly sexual experience. Neither love nor marriage had anything to do with it. Rape did, although Goldman refused to use that word. At the time she was working in a local corset factory. When the workday ended, she always left with a girlfriend, because on most days they could expect to be approached by a young man or two. Together they would walk home, and together they would resist all advances.

One day as the two girls were passing the Hermitage Hotel on their way home, a hotel clerk singled Goldman out for attention. She ignored her potential suitor. But day after day the pattern was repeated until "his perseverance" convinced her to "accept his courtship." Soon the two met after work at a neighborhood pastry shop. For a few months they carried on these clandestine rendezvous without arousing Abraham Goldman's suspicions. But one evening when Goldman returned from the factory having worked "late" yet again, her father refused to believe her. Before she could offer an explanation, he threw her against the shelves of the family grocery store. Enraged, he beat her, all the time shouting that he would not tolerate any more of her behavior or her lies.

Goldman took her punishment without protest, but the experience left her more determined than ever to escape her father's home — and to see the young clerk. The next evening she had just enough time to spill out her story before hurrying home. More short visits followed before the clerk convinced Goldman to go with him into the hotel. After escorting her into one of the rooms, he produced a bottle of wine and asked the girl to "clink glasses in friendship." Before she had begun to sip, he was upon her.

When she regained her composure, Goldman felt no shame — only "shock at the discovery that contact between man and woman could be so brutal and so painful." That sense of shock remained. But for the time being, she told no one of the attack, not even Helena, her one firm ally within the family.

Instead, Goldman retreated within herself, preferring to rely on her own resources, to plot her own escape, and to think her own thoughts. After this violent encounter, she "always felt between two fires in the presence of men. Their lure remained strong, but it was always mingled with violent revulsion."

Of two minds about men in general, Goldman was not at all torn when it came to either her father or her life in St. Petersburg. Sometime during 1885 she had arrived at the conclusion that she must leave both behind her at all costs.

The 1880s were years of growing repression in Russia. A new wave of pogroms swept across the land. The immediate target of official violence was a terrorist organization called the People's Will, some of whose members claimed responsibility for the 1881 assassination of Czar Alexander II. By Taube Goldman's definition, he was the "good czar," who had freed the serfs. Goldman disagreed with her mother without fully knowing why. She had had some contact with St. Petersburg radicals. To her, these alleged terrorists were heroes and victims, not criminals. Years later she conceded that she had been too young to understand the ideological motivations of this rising generation of Russian radicals. Still, a sixteen-year-old Goldman did have thoughts of her own, unformed as they may have been. She knew that "something mysterious had awakened [her] compassion for them," and she did not have a meek bone in her contrary body.

Sometime during her years in St. Petersburg, Goldman came upon a copy of Nikolay Chernyshevsky's influential novel, *What Is to Be Done?* In Chernyshevsky's novel she discovered a heroic woman of independence and power. Vera Pavlovna, a refugee from her class (upper) and her destiny (motherhood), became an ordinary doctor among Russia's poor people. In time, Goldman would attempt a similar mission — even to the point of seeking a medical career of her own. In the meantime, however, she filed away her memory of Vera Pavlovna. Yes, women could have careers. They could dedicate their lives to something other than family members, and they could renounce the conventions of society. Emma Goldman would try to do all of that — and more. But not in Russia.

Life in St. Petersburg had become impossible for Goldman. At home, her father renewed his determination to marry her off and be rid of her for good. In the streets and schools of the city she witnessed the collapse of the radical movement. At some level she knew that she would have to leave Russia to obtain a life of independence and social commitment. But in order to reject her family she also needed help from her family. Helena had already decided to join her sister Lena, who was in the United States. This was Goldman's chance, and she grabbed at it. With Helena's consent (which included her willingness to pay her younger sister's fare), Goldman approached her father. His answer was the expected one: no. Many more no's followed before her threat to leap into the Neva. Only then did he finally relent. Abraham Goldman had had enough.

At that moment, as she contemplated life in America, Goldman knew nothing of the Wobbly Bill Haywood or the socialist Gene Debs or the feminist Margaret Sanger, all American radicals with whom her name would one day be linked. When a few weeks later a frightened sixteen-year-old girl stood inside Castle Garden, on an island near the Battery of New York City, she was thinking less of making a name for herself in America than of making her way to a new life in a new city.

It was somehow appropriate that Goldman's first encounter with America took place in Castle Garden, an imposing old structure that had once served as a concert hall. Much earlier in the century, Jenny Lind, the Swedish nightingale, had performed there. But by 1885 it had been transformed into an entry depot for thousands of immigrants. According to a New York state official, the entire Castle Garden operation had become a "perfect farce." The place had simply been overwhelmed by the numbers of immigrants streaming into the United States.

The immigrants themselves could also be overwhelmed by the experience. Anxiety fed anxiety as they wondered whether they would gain admission. They had to suppress suspicious coughs (inspectors were always alert for tuberculosis, also known as the "Jewish disease") and had to disguise limps as they best they could. (All children over the age of two had to be able to walk by themselves.) They had to undergo unpleasant eye examinations (the suspect, trachoma, accounted for more than half of medical detentions; most of these detainees were Jewish).

Then there were the inevitable questions. Is there insanity in your family? Were you ever in prison? Do you have any money? Is there a job waiting for you?

Goldman found her first day on U.S. soil to be a "violent shock." Nowhere within the "clearinghouse" that was Castle Garden was there a "sympathetic official face." Everywhere there was "antagonism and harshness." The two sisters possessed a single desire—"to escape from the ghastly place" as quickly as possible. Their American dream had begun with a nightmarish prologue.

Rochester, the "Flower City" of New York, would be different—or so the sisters hoped. There family awaited them. There they would find productive jobs in clean factories. There they would be able to earn decent livings and establish new lives. Lena was able to offer the girls shelter, but little more. Pregnant with her first child, she was not anxious to add hungry mouths to an already impossible family budget. She and her husband, who earned twelve dollars a week as a tinsmith, had not been able to establish any cushion for themselves, much less for family members who might find their way to this rapidly industrializing city.

The Rochester of the 1880s was in the midst of tremendous economic and ethnic changes. Originally a city of flour mills, it was by then well on its way to becoming a manufacturing city. Ethnically, it contained communities of Irish, German, and English immigrants. Into this mix came Eastern European Jews, who were initially looked upon as a needed source of cheap labor. By the end of the decade, however, the welcome mat had been removed, and the reality of life in a crowded downtown ghetto had set in. St. Petersburg may have been repressive, but at least it had charm and culture. Rochester may have been a city where some of its citizens could live—or at least dream of living—the American dream, but to a recent arrival from St. Petersburg it was a city of unrelieved congestion and boredom. Soon it revealed its own brand of repression as well.

Goldman's first encounter with factory life in America was in the clothing establishment of a well-appointed German Jewish businessman named Leopold Garson. For him she sewed overcoats for ten and a half hours a day at a wage of two dollars and fifty cents a week. On this money Goldman could satisfy her board and room payments to Lena, but she never had enough left over to satisfy herself. Very quickly she learned the hazards of budgeting for a single factory worker. She also learned that life in America was not necessarily an improvement over life in Russia.

Earlier in U.S. history, factories had relied on the strong backs and nimble fingers of young, unmarried women. Located along the rivers of New England, this first generation of American factories had taken in bales of cotton and armies of farm girls before turning out finished textiles and eligible marital prospects with dowries in hand. It all had made such good sense to the first generation of New England factory owners. They garnered a work force from the surplus daughters of New England farmers. Those same farmers, in turn, were relieved of both financial and parental worries. Their daughters, after all, were to be under a double watch—by foremen on the shop floor and by moral guardians in factory-owned dormitories. The supervision was supposed to be total. Paternalism was the order of the day and night.

By the time Goldman went to work for Garson, the idealism of those early factory owners had disappeared. Garson had not bothered to employ moral shepherds to watch over his flock of hired hands. Had he done so, Goldman no doubt would have done her best to go astray.

Garson, however, did provide Goldman the occasion for a private rebellion. The issue was not the workplace itself— his factory was as spacious and bright as the St. Petersburg glove factory had been cramped and dark. For Goldman the issues were the work itself and its "iron discipline." In the glove factory workers had a lengthy lunch period and two tea breaks. In Garson's model factory the work to Goldman seemed "endless," and the "constant surveillance of the foreman weighed like a stone on my heart." Week after week of "deadly monotony" left her drained. Her brother-in-law's constant grumbling over her contributions to household expenses demanded a solution: She would ask Garson for a raise. Goldman assumed that her case was so compelling that he would have to agree. After all, her wage did not cover all of her basic expenses, much less leave her any money for a book or an occasional theater ticket.

Garson, however, was not impressed. Shielded by an ample desk and wreathed in cigar smoke, he dismissed Goldman's demands and the "extravagant tastes" that fed them. The rest of his workers were content and seemed to be getting along reasonably well. Therefore, Goldman would have to learn to accept her lot or at least do a better job of living within her means—or find work elsewhere.

Within a few days, Goldman had a new job, where she soon met the man who would become her first husband. The factory was smaller, and the discipline in it was minimal. But the pay was higher (four dollars a week), and the young fellow at the adjoining machine was handsome enough to attract Goldman's attention. His name was Jacob Kersner.

Also a Jewish immigrant, Kersner's appeal to Goldman went beyond his good looks to include intellectual pretensions and a self-proclaimed interest in radical politics. Perhaps even more to the point, he offered Goldman a second escape from her parents, who had arrived in Rochester during the early fall of 1886. Abraham and Taube had come to stay. But Goldman had no desire to rekindle those still smoldering family fights. Nor was she excited by the prospect of once again playing the role of full-time daughter. Therefore, the prospect of marriage to Kersner solved immediate problems facing a young girl anxious to establish her independence from a harping brother-in-law and an embittered, controlling father.

On her wedding night, however, Goldman discovered that Kersner's attractiveness could not disguise his impotence. During the ensuing weeks and months she learned that the rest of his life was just as dull and was all too conventional. If he had an obsession it was card playing, not radical politics. Whatever excited him, he was certainly not interested in a sexual life with a new wife who was herself torn between desiring and dreading such a relationship.

Periodic separations led ultimately to divorce. Kersner did not entirely leave Goldman's life, however. Their brief marriage provided her with at least a claim to U.S. citizenship. But for the time being she had grounds for another escape—from Kersner specifically and from marriage generally.

During the fall and winter of 1886–1887, no one new man loomed in Goldman's life. Instead, eight new men claimed her attention and affection—the men charged with the murder of seven Chicago policemen in the Haymarket riot of 1886. They suddenly gave her young life a focus and a depth of commitment it had never had.

Goldman's involvement with these men was strictly vicarious, but it was nonetheless intense. They "saved [her] from utter despair," by playing out their own drama in a Chicago courtroom. Goldman eagerly followed their story in the local press. Throughout the winter of 1886–1887, she kept a close watch over the eight defendants and the appeal of their conviction, the unfairness of which rankled her. None of the men had been charged with throwing a particular bomb or of firing a single gun at any of the 180 policemen sent to contain the Haymarket Square rally, which resulted in a spontaneous outburst of violence and the eventual martrydom of the eight. Throughout the country people followed their story. From the famous (novelist William Dean Howells) to the obscure (immigrant factory worker Goldman), outside observers maintained a prolonged death watch until the execution of four of the eight on November 11, 1887. (Three of the convicted were given substantial prison terms, while one committed suicide a few days before his scheduled execution.)

To Goldman, the suicide victim, Louis Lingg, was her "sublime hero" among the eight. She admired his utter contempt for his accusers and his willpower, "which made him rob his enemies of their prey." Everything about him "lent romance and beauty to his personality." Conversely, everything about the behavior of the state that had tried and condemned Lingg to death pushed Goldman toward her ultimate conviction that the state was the repository of all evil.

Certainly, Goldman's experiences in Russia had pointed her in the general direction of radical politics. Emotionally she was an anarchist of sorts before she ever arrived at Castle Garden. But Haymarket made her stop and think. This episode offered tragic, irrefutable evidence that America was not the paradise that she had anticipated. Anonymous immigration officials, her own brother-in-law, and Leopold Garson had all offered proof that hinted at this disturbing conclusion. But no individual had done to her what the state of Illinois had inflicted on the Haymarket anarchists.

If the state had instigated injustice, anarchism offered to Goldman a new vision of a just society. If the state engaged in calculated demonstrations of power, anarchism promised spontaneous acts of voluntary cooperation. If the state sanctioned inequalities, anarchism stood for a society of equals. And if the state moved to punish those who challenged injustice and inequality, new anarchists had to be ready to fill the depleted ranks.

Goldman was not too young to follow the story of her new heroes as it took them to their graves. All during their ordeal she read whatever she could find concerning the men, the event, the trial, the appeal, and the executions. Among the newspapers she discovered was an anarchist publication, *Die Freiheit*. Its editor was Johann Most, a German immigrant whose frightening demeanor was matched only by his militant prose. Nothing else that Goldman read on the trial or on anarchism captivated her as much as the words of Most. Having devoured "every line of anarchism [she] could get," Goldman was fully ready to join their ranks when she learned that the four had been executed. Their deaths "crystallized my views." Their deaths "made me an active anarchist."

But why anarchism precisely? In the United States of the 1880s and 1890s, all sorts of radicals actively theorized, organized, and propagandized. Greenbackers, single-taxers, and antimonopolists all sought to reduce corporate power by restoring their version of Jeffersonian individualism. Populists embraced a variety of reform measures in the name of aiding the individual farmer, Jeffersonian or not. Union members and their supporters worked for piecemeal reform, including the eight-hour day, to give the American worker an instantly better life. Utopians read Edward Bellamy's *Looking Backward* and endorsed his nationalizing schemes. Socialists combined Bellamy's big government reforms with their support for a good share of the union reform agenda.

Committed anarchists disdained limited reforms that left any vestige of corporate capitalism in place, and they refused to dream socialist dreams that proposed to install an all-powerful central government where capitalism had once been. However, many anarchists had begun their careers as advocates of more limited reforms. Not so Goldman. In fact, her single challenge to American capitalism had not led her to embrace anyone's reform agenda. To hear her tell it, Garson exploited her alone, not workers in general. Therefore, she sought redress alone. She did not organize her sister workers; she did not look to unionization as an answer to her individual problem.

Goldman had attended socialist meetings in Rochester, and she had read some socialist literature. But socialism as an idea was "uninteresting." As a cause it was "colorless," and as a process it was "mechanistic." Only anarchism captured Goldman's fancy. As soon as she embraced it, her life became filled with passion and purpose—in that order. Yes, anarchism held out the promise that society everywhere would be based on justice and reason. But Goldman was also attracted to anarchism because it promised her an exciting life. The prospect of achieving a social order founded on justice and reason was surely enticing, but living a life of high emotional drama was at least as intriguing.

There was little possibility of living such a life as a factory worker in remote Rochester. All the while the Haymarket story swirled in her head, Goldman faced the daily routine of her dull job. Away from the factory she had to contend with the pressures of a failing marriage and of eventual divorce. She might have liked the idea of escape from boredom and oppression in one decisive dart for freedom, but for financial—and perhaps psychological—reasons, that was not possible. Instead she left Rochester in fits and starts.

Not long after the Haymarket executions, Goldman moved to New Haven, Connecticut, where she again worked in a factory to survive. There she made contact with local anarchists, but she also realized that her ties to Rochester were stronger than she had cared to admit. Within a few months she had returned to her first American home. Again she was unhappy. Once again, she married Kersner. The two had officially divorced before Goldman had departed for New Haven. But upon her return, Kersner located her and threatened to commit suicide if she refused to remarry him. She relented, much to her immediate dismay. Again there were sexual difficulties. And again Goldman divorced him before leaving Rochester for good in August 1889.

Almost four years earlier, Goldman had arrived in the United States full of large dreams and frustrated ambitions. Four years later none of her ambitions had been realized. Unable to achieve her goal of becoming a doctor in St. Petersburg, she quickly learned that, for her, school of any sort was impossible in Rochester. Still, she did not abandon her dreams. St. Petersburg she had left behind. Now Rochester would

begin to fade into the past. But a new city loomed before her—
New York City—and an old dream repossessed her. Once she
arrived there, she hoped to be free of her persecutors. There
she would be able to live her own life. There she might even
become a doctor. There she would soon become Emma Goldman, American anarchist.

CHAPTER THREE

In the Streets of America

Twenty-year-old Emma Goldman arrived in New York City on a humid Sunday morning in August carrying everything she owned in the world. With her sewing machine in one hand and a small bag (containing all of five dollars) in the other, she trudged through the Jewish neighborhoods of the East Side. Her destination was Sach's Café on Suffolk Street. Anarchist friends in New Haven had told her that she would find a home there, because the café had a reputation as a gathering place for local radicals. Goldman could barely contain herself as she searched for Suffolk Street. She'd had enough of dull socialist meetings in Rochester. New York City was the center of the radical movement in the East, and her adopted city promised to be anything but dull. For all she knew she might even meet Johann Most at Sach's.

Once she had located the café, Goldman felt right at home among the Russian-, Yiddish-, and German-speaking immigrants gathered at its tables. These were her people. This was already her city.

Before the afternoon was over, Goldman had met a number of East Siders, including an intensely serious young anarchist named Alexander Berkman, who invited her to go with him to hear Most speak that very evening. Within an hour of her arrival in the city, she had found brother and sister anarchists; before the day had ended, she would encounter the two men—Berkman and Most—who would have the greatest impact on these first years of her new life.

In the late 1880s, American radicalism was in a state of ideological and organizational disarray. Those who favored working through the existing political system argued with Marxists and anarchists, who regarded electoral politics as part of the problem, rather than as a step toward any solution. Marxists disagreed among themselves as to whether the day of revolution could be hastened by "direct action" or had to await the development of a mature, committed proletariat. Marxists fought with non-Marxists over the usefulness of working through trade unions to achieve economic reforms.

A wide theoretical gulf separated socialists from anarchists: Socialists believed in both the ballot box and the efficacy of a benevolent and powerful government; anarchists believed in neither. Some socialists accepted immediate reforms, such as the eight-hour workday, as steps in the right direction. Few anarchists, however, agreed with that piecemeal approach. But the differences between the two went beyond matters of tactics and strategy to something more fundamental. Socialism, a Goldman ally once wrote, was simply an "explanation"; anarchism, on the other hand, was, "like all great things, an announcement."

Neither cranks nor eccentrics, anarchists saw themselves as thinkers and activists who carried to "logical ends" tendencies and ideas that already existed in American society. There were crucial differences among those Americans who called themselves anarchists, however. On the one hand were individualist anarchists, led by Benjamin Tucker, who rejected all governmental authority but accepted the legitimacy of private property. Born into a prosperous Massachusetts family, Tucker was a graduate of MIT. In 1881 he began publishing *Liberty*, in which he outlined his defense of private property, which he limited to the land an individual could occupy and use productively. This strand of anarchism had roots in the American experience, traceable at least to the mid-19th century and the writings of Thoreau and Emerson. Adherents claimed to be good Jeffersonians, because they insisted on the primacy of individual liberty over any state-inspired mandate.

During the 1880s, rival anarchists favoring collectivist approaches challenged their individualist counterparts. Largely immigrant in origin, these anarchists opposed both government power and private property. Their goal was a stateless, yet essentially socialist, society composed of small, autonomous cooperatives.

Marxists shared this anarchist vision of one day achieving a condition of perfect statelessness. They disagreed, however, on the means required to achieve this utopia. Marxists believed in the necessity of a transitional period, characterized by an expansion of government authority; hence, the "dictatorship of the proletariat." Anarchists, however, insisted on an immediate move to an absolutely stateless society; hence, their commitment to propaganda. Some anarchists, however, went beyond words to organize conspiratorial groups bent on terror and assassination.

At this early point in the evolution of her anarchist thinking, Goldman was ambivalent on the subject of violence, but vocal in her opposition to the ballot box and piecemeal reform. She also regarded any version of a centralized state as inevitably destructive of personal freedom. Anarchism offered the best of both worlds, because it joined freedom and equality without the corruption of either parliamentary compromises or bureaucratic tangles.

During these formative years in the movement, Goldman was so caught up in the romance and excitement of it all that theoretical precision was a secondary concern. It is safe to say that the young Goldman was consistently closer to the ideal of voluntary cooperatives as pursued by immigrant anarchists than she was to the Tucker wing of the movement. In addition, she quickly came to the conclusion that sexual liberation and sexual equality were essential to her definition of anarchism.

When it came to the desired means, the young Goldman preferred not to make a choice between the "word" (propaganda) and the "deed" (violence). Always a propagandist, she soon flirted with—and occasionally embraced—the glamor of the deed. Never a pacifist, her emphasis on the word should not be taken to mean that she disapproved of all deeds.

violence vs. passivity

Some of Goldman's ambivalence on this critical question can be traced to the two Russian anarchists in her intellectual and personal life: Michael Bakunin and Peter Kropotkin. Bakunin, an imposing figure who paraded across Europe in the 1860s and 1870s, spouted one message: revolution now, revolution forever. In his view the deed was everything, and the goal was a world rid of all oppression. Then, and only then, would it be time to worry about just how to build the utopia to follow.

When Goldman began sorting out her political ideas, she quickly decided that Bakunin was someone to regard highly. Marx was "hopelessly middle class" in comparison. But her choice was not simply between Bakunin and Marx. As an anarchist, she was caught between Bakunin and Kropotkin. A geographer by training, Kropotkin was the exact opposite of Bakunin. Where the impulsive Bakunin preached violence, the thoughtful Kropotkin counseled passivity. Where Bakunin told his followers to seize the moment, Kropotkin cautioned his readers to think carefully about the world they desired to create before they destroyed the one in which they actually lived in.

Bakunin blithely assumed that blowing up the old order and clearing away its debris would ensure the triumph of the new. Kropotkin, on the other hand, invested a great deal of intellectual energy in planning his new order. Behind his thinking was a working assumption both supremely simple and grandly idealistic: Because there was no conflict between the interests of the individual and those of society, there was no need for private property. People naturally had a common urge to cooperate. Out of this drive would eventually emerge small communes, provided that the twin corruptions of governmental power (in all its forms) and Bakuninist revolutionaries (in all their fervor) could be kept in check.

Kropotkin's theory of voluntaristic cooperation rubbed up against popular Social Darwinist notions, which held that individual and societal progress depended on competition. Like

Social Darwinists, Kropotkin believed in progress—and in evolution—but he did not think that either had roots in notions of "survival of the fittest." Instead, he offered his concept of "mutual aid" as both more rational and as a closer reflection of human nature. These ideas had genuine appeal to immigrants who believed in the American dream, but who had come to feel cheated by their American experiences.

Goldman was among those immigrants. At times, she was critical of Kropotkin's aloof, almost dour personality. He, in turn, let it be known within anarchist circles that he disapproved of her chaotic private life. Still, she increasingly pointed to Kropotkin as her teacher and guide to the future. She accepted, without dissent, his outline of a world based on communal anarchism.

Over time, Goldman's reverence for the gentle Kropotkin grew, even if she seldom shared his admiration for—and confidence in—"the people." Goldman, impatient at any age, could not wait for the masses to see the wisdom of her point of view. On this score, she was closer to Bakunin than Kropotkin. Moreover, like Bakunin, she was always more inclined to embrace the romance of revolt than to work out the fine details of any utopia. Condemning the present was her stock in trade; imagining the future was not.

Nonetheless, Bakunin and Kropotkin remained at odds within Goldman's heart and head. Temperamentally, the youthful Goldman was a Bakuninite. Intellectually, the more mature Goldman found Kropotkin's ideas more appealing. Never would she give herself entirely to one or the other.

Goldman also fell somewhere between the communistic and individualistic strands of anarchism. As an immigrant and an anarchist, she should have cast her lot with the communal ideal. Generally she did. When she thought at all of her utopia, she posited a kind of Kropotkin village. Yet she found much in common with American anarchists who were individualists when it came to both economic and civil libertarian questions. She admired their outspoken defense of personal freedom, their tenacious opposition to censorship, and their unchanging hatred of the state—especially its military arm.

Political animal that she was, Goldman must have also sensed that an identification with the heroes of these anarchist-individualists—with Jefferson and Thoreau and Emerson—would provide her with an entrée to the mass of working-class and middle-class Americans.

But in August 1889, Goldman's first order of business was to gain the acceptance of the East Side immigrant radicals. After her arrival in New York City, she began to sort out the anarchists from the socialists—a considerable undertaking all its own. Separating some anarchists from others would have to wait a few years.

Unlike Thoreau, when Goldman thought about anarchism in 1889, she did not have the benefit of spending a quiet afternoon near Walden Pond. She could not walk the shaded streets of Concord with Emerson, much less visit Jefferson in gracious retirement at Monticello. In 1889, Goldman was willing to think and to learn about anarchism, but she wanted to act as well. Her immediate teachers were two fellow immigrants: the speechmaker on that Sunday evening in August, Johann Most, and her escort from Sach's Café, Alexander Berkman.

German born, Most had come to the United States in 1883 after a four-year exile in London. Gripped by bitterness, Most was a volcano of a man, whose eruptions were frequent and fierce. Illegitimate at birth and orphaned at nine, he grew into a man of raging hatreds and impossible dreams. He despised his past but determined to overcome it through a career in the theater. Even as a youth he had the makings of an actor—despite his height, which never stretched beyond five feet four inches. His voice was magnificent, and his presence could be commanding. Yet a stage career escaped him. One irremediable defect stood athwart his path to theatrical greatness: a disfigured face, the result of a childhood infection and botched surgery. It was almost as though he had knowingly selected a craft at which he had little chance for success.

Most covered his deformed face with a beard, but he could not hide his anger at a world that had dealt him so many harsh blows. Radical politics, in part, offered an outlet for his personal rage. For ten years he was a socialist agitator in Germany.

Imprisoned twice for his radical views, he left Germany for London in 1878. There he began to publish *Die Freiheit* before being jailed again, this time for writing an editorial praising the assassination of Czar Alexander II of Russia.

Upon his release in 1882, Most accepted an invitation from American socialists to visit New York City, where he immediately thought he had set foot on fertile territory for his ideas and ambitions. Taking residence in the city, he revived *Die Freiheit* and rapidly made a name for himself in American radical circles. In 1883 radicals, including anarchists, socialists, and Marxists, gathered in Pittsburgh to bring some semblance of unity to their quarrelsome ranks. Most not only helped to organize the conference, but he dominated it with his unique blend of the Kropotkin and Bakuninite positions. In the process, he alienated Marxists, who objected to his call for a series of decentralized communities, as well as individualist anarchists and socialists, who were horrified by his advocacy of violence and sabotage. The Pittsburgh Manifesto, penned essentially by Most, in fact endorsed the use of violence to bring down the existing social order. In the years immediately following, Most continued to state his case for the "deed," even to the point of printing instructions for making bombs and other explosives.

Largely through Most's efforts, anarchist ranks in America grew significantly during the 1880s. Perhaps as many as 7,000 people called themselves anarchists by the end of the decade. Not all of them were necessarily believers in the "deed," but many did read *Die Freiheit,* and a good percentage of those surely looked to Most for leadership. But Most soon proved to be an autocrat of the worst sort. While claiming to hate all forms of authority, he established himself as a leader who could be as doctrinaire, as humorless, and as dictatorial as any of his capitalist enemies.

By 1889, after rival Chicago anarchists had been decimated by the consequences of Haymarket, the center of American anarchism had shifted to New York City, where Most reigned supreme. When he was not antagonizing the city's conservative establishment through the pages of *Die Freiheit,* he was working the Lower East Side, where he harangued—and captivated—audiences with his fiery words and steely glare. On a hot Sunday night in August, his ideas and his rhetoric combined to bring Emma Goldman within his circle of admirers.

Goldman's companion that evening was a young disciple of Most's. Then nineteen, Alexander Berkman had migrated to the United States from Russia in early 1888. In the intervening year and a half he had worked as a cigarmaker and a cloakmaker before securing work as a printer for Most's *Die Freiheit*.

Berkman's relationship with Goldman would survive until his death in 1936. During those nearly fifty years, they would be lovers and co-conspirators. For extended periods within that long span they would be separated—by prison walls and by other loves. For brief periods they would fight, sometimes through the mail and sometimes face-to-face. But always they would be friends and allies.

Theirs was a relationship of equals. Each could rely on the other without falling into the trap of permanent dependence. Each could learn from the other without assuming a fixed role as student or teacher. And each always knew that the other was a crucial person in his or her life. To Berkman, Goldman was the one "immutable" he could count on. To Goldman, Berkman was alternately a source of strength and an object of compassion.

Sometimes Goldman thought that Berkman was too obsessed with revolution, too much the fanatic, too severely the puritan. In turn, he often dismissed her as frivolous and unserious, as someone too reluctant to pursue the "cause" or commit the "deed." In their dealings with each other, however, these two anarchists strove to practice the equality that they preached.

The two had much in common when they met in Sach's Café. Although Berkman grew up in a more bourgeois family, he, too, rapidly learned to hate his father, who was as materialistic as Goldman's father was vindictive. Both spent their formative adolescent years in St. Petersburg. Both were deeply influenced by Chernyshevksy's *What Is to Be Done?* Even though both were too young to participate fully in the Russian nihilist movement, both hovered around its fraying edges. Neither, however, was too young to rebel against traditional schooling, and neither was able to resist the migration to America, where both rapidly gravitated to the anarchist movement before either had reached the age of twenty.

Not long after they had met, Goldman and Berkman became lovers. With two other young women, they organized a commune in an apartment on 42nd Street. Goldman established herself as the housekeeper, while Berkman shared his time between a cigar factory and *Die Freiheit*. The two of them argued endlessly over revolutionary ethics. To Berkman, the true revolutionary had to sacrifice everything for the cause. To Goldman, the true revolution had to be a liberating experience for everyone, participants and nonparticipants alike. Revolutionaries should not have to surrender the finer things of life, and revolutions should be concerned with more than promoting social and economic equality. Personal liberation, Goldman insisted, should be the goal of all true revolutionaries. To her, a liberated life meant a life filled with the beauty of theater, dance, music, and sexuality. To Berkman, such "luxuries" stood in the way of his pursuit of the cause.

Not that Goldman ignored the coming social revolution. When she was not cooking for her foursome or making silk shirtwaists out of their apartment, she was learning public speaking from Most. When she was not busy refining her forensic techniques, she was organizing immigrant workers in the city's garment district. However, none of these enterprises satisfied her during her early months as a New York radical.

Most had promised Goldman that he would make her a public speaker. For weeks he worked with her, filling her head with the necessity for direct action, including violence, and teaching her his platform skills. He convinced his student that the "spoken word," if "hurled forth" with "eloquence, enthusiasm, and fire, could never be erased from the human soul." From that first night in August, Goldman knew what she wanted. Captivated by Most the performer, she was determined to be a performer herself.

True to his promise, in the late winter of 1890 Most sent his newest protégée on a speaking tour that took her across New York state as far west as Cleveland, Ohio. Almost immediately, Goldman became aware of her considerable power as a speaker. At an appearance in Rochester, "words I had never heard myself utter [came] pouring forth, faster and faster." It was as though she was a woman possessed: "The audience had vanished, the hall itself had disappeared; I was conscious only of my own words, of my ecstatic song." The result was a kind of revelation: "I could sway people with words! Strange and magic words that welled up within me, from some unfamiliar depth." However, her instructions from Most were not to break into "ecstatic songs," not to permit words to control her, but to preach his line, to urge her listeners to bring down the old order, to embrace revolution and to repudiate reform.

At this point, the crucial issue that divided radicals from reformers was whether to endorse the eight-hour workday. Goldman was under strict orders to state Most's case against this reform, which he regarded as a smoke screen distracting workers from the larger struggle against capitalism. In his view, the eight-hour day diverted the troops from the real fight by promising the obvious: a shorter workday (at a time when workweeks of 60 to 70 hours were still common), with the prospect of greater opportunities for leisure and recreation (at a time when such commodities were scarce for American workers).

The American Federation of Labor had already endorsed the eight-hour workday. Willing to work hand in hand with capitalists, the AFL anticipated that a better life could be bargained for within the confines of capitalism. The Knights of Labor, a dying national union, had spurned such thinking. In one sense, Most agreed with the Knights. Both opposed the eight-hour workday because it would make workers too comfortable in their stations. But the ends they sought to achieve were not congruent. The Knights looked to a day when capitalism would be universal. Most labored to advance the day when capitalism would be no more.

Goldman had no difficulty accepting either Most's conclusion or the reasoning he used to get there. She, too, wanted an end to the evil (rather than just the evils) of capitalism. She understood that the eight-hour workday represented no real gain for workers. In fact, the result would be far worse: workers' muscles might rest, but their minds would be diverted from the real issue—the elimination of capitalism.

As she made her way west, Goldman preached this gospel tirelessly. Not until Cleveland did she receive any challenge. An elderly worker approached her at the end of her talk. What were men and women of my age to do, he asked, while they awaited the day that they would never live to see? Why must he work such long hard days in this interim period that had no foreseeable end? This anarchists' society of the future might be wonderful indeed, he conceded. "But what about right now? What was so wrong with wanting a better life today?"

Goldman was stunned by the directness and simplicity of this argument. She quickly saw the logic, even the justice, in what the man had to say. Why should he have to sacrifice something of immediate benefit so that nameless, faceless workers at some point in an unknown future could live in a world without artificial divisions of workers and owners?

To complicate matters, Goldman came to a second conclusion no more reassuring than the first. On this, her baptismal tour as a spokeswoman for anarchism, she was merely parroting Most's gospel to the masses. She thought she believed it, but she retreated the first time she was seriously questioned—not because she was meek or submissive, but because she had instantly seen the weakness in Most's line of argument.

Still convinced that she wanted to continue to speak, but now determined to think for herself on the platform, Goldman returned to New York City to have a talk with Most. She told him the story of her Cleveland exchange. Then she let him know exactly what she had learned from the experience: On the eight-hour workday issue, the old worker was right. From that day forward Goldman would do her own thinking and speaking.

Most refused to accept Goldman's new terms. She was his creation. He had trained her and had filled her head with his ideas. Therefore, he lashed out at her in a manner that she recognized but had never seen directed at her. Insubordination would not be tolerated: "Who is not with me is against me." At fifteen, Goldman had refused to accept her father's rules; at nearly twenty-one, she had no intention of living by Most's commands. With few regrets, and with genuine admiration for his fervor and honestly held convictions, Goldman left Most's anarchist army for an uncertain but more independent future.

As early as 1890, Goldman found herself moving toward a rival anarchist circle in New York City, led by Joseph Peukert. Publisher of his own anarchist weekly, *Die Autonomie,* Peukert was closer to Kropotkin than to Bakunin. Within his circle of followers, individual freedom within a communal setting counted more than dictatorial control over an enforced community. At his meetings autonomy, not autocrats, ruled.

Autonomy was important to Goldman, especially when she found out that Most expected total subservience and had decided to make his student his lover as well. She did not welcome the news of his sexual interest in her. A radical in the streets but a traditionalist in the home, Most wanted someone to be his wife and the mother of his children. Goldman had no interest in assuming either role—with Most or with anyone else. She had just begun to enjoy her freedom and had only commenced what would be a lifelong process of exploring her own sexuality. She saw Most only as a stern father figure. Finally, she did not find Most physically attractive, and he reacted jealously to the mutual attraction between Berkman and Goldman.

All the while that Most fumed and plotted, Goldman and Berkman loved each other and collaborated in the name of anarchy. Unlike Most, Berkman recognized his own possessive tendencies when it came to women. He could permit Goldman her own "freedom to love," a freedom she then saw no reason to assert.

Together the two made quite a pair on the streets of New York City, as they organized workers, led strikes, and trumpeted the joys of communal living to anyone who would listen.

But after nearly three years, they decided that they had had enough. The revolution had invaded neither the streets nor the bedrooms of the city. Therefore, the time had come for Berkman, at least, to return to his native Russia to work for the revolution there. To raise money for the journey, he and Goldman decided to join ranks with the hated capitalists. In New Haven, she tried to organize a cooperative dressmaking shop, while he chose to continue working in printing. When her venture failed, the two opened a photography studio in Worcester, Massachusetts, where customers proved as scarce as converts to anarchism.

Professed anarchists, Goldman and Berkman became practicing capitalists. Despite repeated setbacks, they pressed on. Lesser capitalists might have given up, but not these two, who were then so new to the game. Besides, they needed to earn money quickly. Atrocities against their Russian compatriots, Jews and anarchists alike, had convinced them that they should return to Russia to live and work as revolutionaries.

Moving on to a new venture, Goldman and Berkman opened an ice-cream parlor in Worcester. This time they were on their way to making money—and, they hoped, to Russia. To their great surprise, they were a success. Operating what must have been the only anarchist-run ice-cream shop in all of New England, Goldman inadvertently discovered the secret of high-volume selling.

Goldman's first thoughts were for ice-cream loving children, few of whom had so much as a single coin to spend on ice cream. For those who did, Goldman beneficently dished up double scoops for the single-scoop price. In the short run, she lost money; in the slightly longer run, her benevolence created enough new customers to assure the couple's eventual return to Russia. Just at that point, when the ice-cream anarchists were dangerously close to turning a necessary, if tainted, profit, Goldman spied a newspaper headline that hinted at disturbing labor news in Homestead, Pennsylvania.

In May 1892, the Carnegie Steel Company and the Amalgamated Association of Iron and Steel Workers stood on the verge of open warfare. The existing contract between the company and the union had expired. The main issue revolved around the union's desire to retain, but amend, a sliding wage scale then based on the prevailing market price of steel products. Carnegie and his chief lieutenant, Henry Clay Frick, ultimately wanted to do away with both the sliding scale and the union. Immediately, they sought to institute an 18 percent wage cut, owing to a drop in the price of steel billets. In response, the workers demanded a new wage scale based on steel production, rather than its price. In Goldman's eyes these union workers were men of "decision and grit," men who did not hesitate to "assert their rights."

Just as decisive and just as gritty—and just as determined to uphold their position—Carnegie and Frick had no intention of backing down. They answered the union challenge by breaking off negotiations and imposing a lockout. Following this action, Frick hired some 300 Pinkerton guards to clear the way for the reopening of a nonunion Homestead steel plant. To accommodate the Pinkertons, he ordered the construction of a three-mile barricade, drilled with gun sights and festooned with barbed wire.

Business as usual was scheduled to resume on July 6. Instead, war erupted the next day. In the ensuing battle, three Pinkertons and ten workers were killed. Despite the casualties, the striking workers routed the hapless Pinkertons, a last group of whom ran a gauntlet of furious union wives brandishing socks filled with jagged steel fragments.

The workers and their wives won the battle but lost the war. Frick emerged from the smoke and the steel shards with his wage cut intact and the union in shambles. Carnegie was nowhere to be found. It seems that Scotland beckoned, while Homestead burned.

The defeat of the Pinkertons did little to dampen the fury of radicals who could not ignore the reality of a private army hired to kill workers and break their union. Goldman and Berkman instantly decided to join those angry radicals. To go on blithely selling confectioneries in New England seemed ludicrous, and a return to Russia suddenly made no sense. The "long-awaited day of resurrection" (for the American worker) had finally arrived; Russia would have to wait. For Goldman, the decision was a simple one: "We belonged in Homestead."

Before Goldman and Berkman could leave for Homestead—before they could even think about shutting down their ice-cream parlor—they had to argue. Berkman had no doubt that he should be among the oppressed steelworkers, and he insisted that Goldman return to New York. He would be the man of action. In fact, he alone would go to Pittsburgh to kill Frick. She had a duty to remain behind to tell the world about his "deed." Her talent for propaganda dictated that she provide the "word"; he should perform the act. Berkman's arbitrary division of labor did not please Goldman at all. But, uncharacteristically, she gave up the fight.

As a first step, Goldman and Berkman turned over the day's receipts—all seventy-five dollars—to their astonished landlord as settlement for back rent. Double-scoop time in Worcester ended abruptly as the two shut their doors and jumped aboard the next train for New York.

Berkman did not intend to be entirely alone on the next leg of his journey to western Pennsylvania. Accompanying him would be a homemade time bomb. A week of feverish tinkering and a wasted forty dollars produced nothing to detonate, however. "Wet dynamite" was the apparent problem.

Down to their last few dollars, the two accomplices decided that Berkman should leave for Pittsburgh anyway. Meanwhile, Goldman would remain in New York to raise money for a new suit of clothes (the better to gain access to Frick's inner sanctum) and a revolver. But how could she earn money quickly? Her only answer was to take to the streets as a prostitute. Lying in bed pondering her alternatives, she recalled a character from Dostoyevski's *Crime and Punishment* who had become a prostitute to support her younger brothers and sisters. If "sensitive Sonya could sell her body; why not I? My cause was greater than hers." The thought revolted her. "Weakling, coward," an inner voice admonished. "Sasha is giving his life, and you shrink from giving your body, miserable coward!"

Thus began Goldman's brief career as a prostitute. Her first and only patron was an elderly gentleman who suspected that

Goldman had selected the wrong line of work. Having observed her for a time trudging along with her rival solicitors, he invited her into a nearby saloon, where he promptly bought her a beer, gave her ten dollars, and advised her to give up on a career she obviously had no "knack" for.

An embarrassed Goldman was "too astounded for speech," but she recovered in time to suggest that perhaps she still ought to earn her money. He demurred, then departed, but not without leaving the ten dollars in Goldman's hands.

A good suit of clothes and a revolver cost far more than the ten dollars Goldman had "earned." In a pinch, she always knew that she could count on Helena, who subsequently agreed to make up the difference—no questions asked. When Berkman subsequently wired for money, Goldman was able to send him what he needed.

Using the alias of Simon Bachman, president of a fictitious agency of strikebreakers, Berkman gained admittance to Frick's office on the afternoon of Saturday, July 23. Suddenly two of the most driven and contrary men of that era were face-to-face. As inflexible as the steel that his mills produced, Frick had not achieved his lofty station by bending to the demands of his workers. But when Berkman stood before him brandishing his cheap revolver, Frick had no opportunity to negotiate.

What follows are Berkman's own words: "There is a flash, and the high-ceilinged room reverberates as with the booming of a cannon. I hear a sharp piercing cry, and see Frick on his knees . . . He is lying head and shoulders under the large armchair, without sound or motion. 'Dead?' I wonder. I must make sure."

Berkman managed to fire two more shots before a company carpenter burst into the room and knocked him to the floor. In the ensuing struggle Berkman pulled a dagger from his pocket and thrust it repeatedly into Frick's legs. He heard Frick "cry out in pain," but before he could inflict any more damage, he was subdued and "lifted bodily from the floor." Through it all, Frick remained conscious and in command, even to the point of insisting that Berkman not be harmed, so that the law would be allowed to take its course.

Berkman, however, did not intend to give the judicial system a chance to work its will. If caught, he planned to kill himself, to make a "voluntary anarchist self-sacrifice," thereby linking himself to the European terrorists of the 1870s and 1880s he deeply admired. His attempted suicide was foiled. The day after his attack on Frick, a guard discovered Berkman chewing what proved to be a capsule of poison, which was forcibly removed before it could do its work. Unable to follow the example of his Haymarket hero, Louis Lingg, Berkman then decided that his demise would have to take place after he had explained the "purpose of my act" at a trial.

The trial proved a farce. When Berkman first appeared in court, he discovered that the jury had already been selected. He served as his own attorney, but his closing speech—translated from German and read by a blind incompetent—was cut off by the judge a third of the way through. Spared further indignities, Berkman, failed assassin, failed self-exterminator, and failed defense counsel, received a sentence of twenty-one years in Western Penitentiary, to be followed by one year in the Allegheny Workhouse.

To make matters worse, Most publicly speculated that Berkman's attack had been staged for the sole purpose of gaining sympathy for Frick. With Goldman herself in his New York audience, Most went on to condemn individual acts of terrorism as impractical and immature. Goldman was stunned. These were the very acts that *Die Freiheit* had advocated, and Most himself had preached the virtues of violence. Now he ridiculed someone who had acted courageously on that command and had the effrontery to stand before her and reveal himself to be an unconscionable hypocrite.

Goldman challenged Most to prove his first point and accused him of cowardice for making his second. Unconcerned, Most refused her so much as the courtesy of a response. He should have known better than to think that Goldman was through with him. At his very next lecture, Most repeated his charges before again spurning a direct confrontation with his accuser. This time Goldman leaped to the podium, pulled a horsewhip from beneath her cloak, and furiously lashed Most across the face before finally breaking the whip over her knee and throwing the pieces at his feet.

If Goldman needed a dramatic break with Most, this moment certainly met any requirements. If an enforced separation from Berkman was unavoidable, she could deal with that, too. In the meantime, she would carry on their struggle. She would stay on the front lines to give meaning to his act—and, possibly, to compensate for her unpunished role in it.

Goldman decided immediately to take to the lecture circuit on her own. Much work remained to be done, especially if ordinary working people violated their class interests by rushing to the aid of tyrants such as Frick. A few years earlier, financier Jay Gould had publicly boasted that he could "hire half the working class to kill the other half." In 1892, Goldman worried that he may well have been right.

In her spare time away from the speaker's platform, Goldman devoted herself to Berkman, to defending his deed, to assisting him in his plans for escape. He was amazed, but gratified, by her loyalty. At times anger flashed between the two. She accepted the "burden of responsibility" for his welfare with some resentment. Occasionally, she reminded him that she, too, had suffered, that she, too, had made sacrifices—for him and for their cause.

Goldman, after all, had defended Berkman's act at a time when he needed defenders. Kropotkin joined Most and other anarchists in attacking Berkman for a deed that would only delay the ultimate triumph of anarchism by giving the state an excuse for repression.

All this made Goldman even more determined to rally behind Berkman and to portray all political assassins as historical actors with superior courage. Never did she publicly endorse assassination as such. Privately, she may well have discouraged any number of would-be assassins from actually picking up the gun. But for many years to come she could not bring herself to condemn those who did. She thought Berkman deserved as much.

In the meantime, Berkman marveled at Goldman's fierce loyalty and contemplated plans for escape. Even though both doubted that American workers would help hide and shelter him, Goldman vowed to help Berkman if he requested it. Entitled to one visit a month, and that only from a close relative, Berkman asked that his "sister" from Russia come to the prison. Understanding the message at once, she decided to combine a trip to Chicago commemorating the Haymarket affair with a stop at Western Penitentiary "to see my boy again." The visit, however, only added to her agony. They were forbidden to speak for longer than twenty minutes, at which point an iron gate "clattered shut" behind her. A second visit was quashed when the authorities discovered that "Mrs. Niedermann," the criminal's sister, was in fact Goldman, the criminal's lover. The officials permitted no more visits and allowed no more plots to be hatched. In response, Goldman threatened to kill the accusing official "with my own hands." She settled, eventually, for destroying a tray of watches in his jewelry shop before leaving Pittsburgh. Any conspiracies, legal or otherwise, to secure Berkman's release would have to be undertaken from a distance.

When Goldman's anger cooled, she took time to think about Berkman's act, anarchist dissension over it, and the revolutionary fervor (or lack thereof) of the American working class. During this brief hiatus, she made a crucial decision. Worker resistance aside, she resolved to make her stand in the United States. More than that, she decided to concentrate her propaganda efforts among nonimmigrant workers. They were the ones who had to be made into good radicals. Therefore, she vowed that she would no longer speak exclusively in German and Yiddish to small knots of recent arrivals to the American working class.

Within a year of Homestead, Goldman's new commitment to a more broadly based American radicalism led to friendships with reformers outside the narrow world of the immigrant anarchists and the equally compressed world of American socialism. She made contact with settlement house workers in New York City, including Lillian Wald of Henry Street. Although Wald had little use for anarchism, she shared Goldman's concern for the downtrodden. One of the worst economic crises in American history gripped the nation in 1893. By midyear, an estimated 800,000 workers were unemployed.

Six months later that figure had climbed to at least 3 million. Through the summer and fall, the unemployed grew angrier. Riots spontaneously erupted in the streets of New York. Labor leaders became more outspoken in their demands for government relief. In fact, as the depression deepened, some even talked about marching on Washington itself.

At the same time, feminists within and without the settlement houses urged Goldman to join in their demand for the vote, a step she could not take. To her, suffrage was a bourgeois invention that simply played into the hands of those who knew how to block economic and social change. Suffragists disagreed. To them, the vote was a matter of simple equality and an opportunity to effect wider social reform. Goldman, however, continued to keep her distance from those feminists who insisted that "all that was needed was independence from external tyrannies" (such as a male-only voter list). In her view, the "internal tyrants" were just as important to exorcise. Never could she believe that all women's problems would be solved once their "external realities" had been rearranged.

But in the midst of the depression year of 1893, "external realities" oppressed the poor, whatever their gender. The unemployed and the poor needed food. Speaking (this time in German) at a hunger demonstration August 18, Goldman reportedly urged her listeners to "go and get" bread if they were hungry. She told them that the "shops are plentiful and the doors are open." Three days later, she spoke to a crowd of some 3,000 in Union Square, including more than a few policemen. There, between barbs at socialists and their mild public works programs, she again urged the unemployed to take matters into their own hands.

Goldman's precise words at the Union Square rally will never be known. Undercover detectives later insisted that she had instructed her listeners to "take everything" and take it "by force." Goldman contended that she had merely counseled the unemployed to demand food from the wealthy directly, rather than to turn to the government for relief of any sort. The question remained: Had she called for demonstrations or expropriations? Ultimately a court would decide.

On August 30 police arrested Goldman in Philadelphia and returned her to New York for indictment and trial. This turn of events fazed Goldman but slightly. Now she had a chance to be one with Berkman. She could make a name for herself as an anarchist leader and advocate of the unemployed. Previously, she had kept her distance from reporters. Now she courted them.

Nelly Bly of the New York *World* spent two hours with Goldman in prison listening to her tale. The result was a front-page story on this "saucy" young woman with a "turned-up nose" and a "seriousness of purpose." To Bly, Goldman was a "little Joan of Arc," who "loved good books" and wanted only "justice and freedom of speech" for everyone. Goldman could not have asked for better coverage had she written the story herself.

The trial itself proved another story. A former mayor of New York City, A. Oakley Hall, defended Goldman without charge. More intent on exposing police corruption than in securing his client's release, Hall failed miserably on both counts. The highlight of the trial was Goldman's decision to take the stand in her own defense. There she answered questions at length about everything from anarchism in general to Berkman's role in her life to her exact words on August 21. In response, she insisted that she had only advised the unemployed to demonstrate. Her story did not suit the judge or the jury. After a five-day trial, she was found guilty of "inciting a riot," even though there had been no riot on August 21. A few days later the presiding judge sentenced her to a year in prison.

But what *had* Goldman said? In her memoirs, written better than thirty years after the incident, Goldman recalled throwing away her notes and speaking from her heart. What follows is her own reconstruction of her final words on this August evening in Union Square:

> You, too will have to learn that you have a right to share your neighbor's bread. Your neighbors—they have not only stolen your bread, but they are sapping your blood. They

will go on robbing you, your children, and your children's children, unless you wake up, unless you become daring enough to demand your rights. Well, then, demonstrate before the palaces of the rich; demand work. If they do not give you work, demand bread. If they deny both, take bread. It is your sacred right!

A call for demonstrations or a demand for expropriations? Whatever her exact words, she would soon have plenty of time to ponder them. Emma Goldman, agitator, was about to become Emma Goldman, prisoner.

CHAPTER FOUR

Jail . . . and After

❖
❖

On the very day of her sentence, Goldman entered Black-well's Island Penitentiary. A dumping ground for many of New York's unwanted, this small plot of land contained a lunatic asylum, an almshouse, and a smallpox hospital. There the insane, the impoverished, and the diseased were quarantined with the convicted. There Goldman was scheduled to spend the next year of her life.

When she walked through the heavy prison gates, Goldman was expected to work to earn her keep. Having reluctantly enlisted in the army of America's female factory workers, she was about to learn the routine and culture of one more American institution. From Garson's clothing factory to Blackwell's Island was not a straight line. Too much had happened in between. But there was a certain irony—and symmetry—to Goldman's story during her first years in the United States. An anarchist distrustful of all institutions, she found herself confined once again. An anarchist disdainful of class-based benevolence, she was about to acquire confirming evidence of its failures.

Put in charge of the prison's sewing room, Goldman the seamstress did not appreciate this attempt at job placement on the part of her enemy, the state. Here she was, not yet eight years in America, and the state had found an excuse to jail her. More than that, the state was forcing her to do its bidding, to work by getting work out of her sister inmates.

Initially, those inmates did not trust her—and with some reason. One of her more onerous tasks was to monitor their production, to account for all bundles of cloth entering and leaving her room. Moreover, Goldman came to that sewing room with a reputation. She was an anarchist; therefore, she was an unbeliever. She refused to attend church; therefore, she deserved to be shunned—or so grumbled some of her underlings, although not for long.

Recalling her own treatment at the hands of foremen, Goldman declined to play a similar role, even at the risk of punishment by her superiors. When the head matron demanded that she force her charges to work harder, she simply refused. For her punishment she was assigned to be an orderly in the prison hospital, a sensible decision whether her keepers knew it or not. Goldman had long been interested in medicine. Here was a chance to practice it without a license.

Before she began her new job, Goldman became a patient when an attack of rheumatism downed her. Confined to bed for a month, she emerged ready to minister to her sister patients. Within a few weeks she had assumed responsibility for the entire hospital ward. One of her daily tasks was to divide food rations. Each day every hospitalized inmate received one quart of milk, a cup of beef tea, two eggs, two crackers, and two lumps of sugar. On more than one occasion the milk and the eggs were missing from the menus of some of the prisoners, particularly those who happened to be Jewish or Irish. When Goldman reported these peculiar omissions to the head matron, she was summarily told that those patients were "strong enough to do without their *extra* rations." Later Goldman discovered that the head matron was giving the missing portions to "two husky Negro prisoners," whom she had been grooming as her personal eyes and ears within the institution. Angered by this example of discrimination, she was frustrated by her "powerlessness" to alter the practice.

Goldman's sense of frustration mounted the following spring, when Blackwell's Island received a large number of prostitutes. Were the men caught in these "public houses" arrested as well? she asked the startled warden. "No," was his casual reply.

The new inmates arrived in a "deplorable condition," made instantly worse by their inability to obtain the narcotics they had grown accustomed to. These "frail creatures," recalled Goldman, suddenly acquired the "strength of giants," as they shook their bars in the vain hope that their demands would be met. For years prior to her own imprisonment, Goldman had often smoked "as many as forty cigarettes a day." For stretches of time she actually preferred smoking to eating. In prison, however, she could not satisfy her habit. The "torture" was "almost beyond endurance," but somehow she forgot her craving in reading.

When the new inmates learned that Goldman was the guardian of the medicine chest, they offered her money and badgered her: "Just a whiff of dope, for the love of Christ!" Goldman would not relent. She despised the "Christian hypocrisy" that imprisoned women for selling their sexual favors to men who were never jailed for their part of the bargain, and she thought it ruthless to deny these women the narcotics that many of them had used for years. But the doctor who had entrusted her with the distribution of medicine had ordered her not to provide the desired "whiffs of dope" for any purpose, even medicinal. He had placed his faith in her; he had been "kind and generous—I could not fail him." Goldman was seldom loyal to institutions, but she could be very loyal to individuals, even individuals of authority, if they had been loyal to her.

Many of the prison authorities came to admire Goldman's talents as a caretaker. According to the warden, she went about her daily routines with a "tender touch and a sympathetic smile." So willing was she to give her time that Goldman gradually took on a second career. Nurse Goldman became Counselor Goldman, a confidante to "poor creatures" hungry for the "least sign" of kindness. She raised that sign by extending herself. Having done so, she discovered that her sister inmates were willing to bring their "troubles" to her.

Despite her long days, Goldman found time to read and receive visitors. For the first time she read extensively, in English, the works of Emerson, Thoreau, Hawthorne, and Whitman. This was her chance to improve her English and at the same time learn more about the American libertarian tradition. Benjamin Tucker's heroes were not yet her heroes, but she was at least able to acquaint herself with the intellectual roots of the branch of American anarchism that placed the highest of values on individual freedom.

Goldman appreciated Thoreau in particular. The solitude of Walden Pond was far removed from the bustle of New York City, and the angular, reflective New Englander did not at all resemble the squat, outspoken Jewish immigrant. But Thoreau's fierce independence was matched by that of the young woman who read him during what proved to be her ten months in jail.

Books were important to Goldman, but not as important as people. Fortunately, her prison duties required daily contact with many people. At the same time, she was permitted to receive visitors. Blackwell's Island was close enough to Manhattan so that a number of her allies made the short pilgrimage to her. Included among the pilgrims was one John Swinton. During his younger days he, too, claimed the label radical. As an abolitionist his speeches had been more violent than anything Goldman had uttered in Union Square. No anarchist, Swinton in 1893 was the editor-in-chief of the New York *Sun* and a self-appointed advocate of the rights of immigrants. To him, Goldman's imprisonment was a travesty, and anyone who participated in holding this "little girl" on Blackwell's Island "ought to be ashamed."

The warden assured Swinton that Goldman was a "model prisoner." In fact, she was such a wonderful prisoner that he wished she'd been "sentenced to a five-year term," because good nurses were hard to find.

"Then why not give her a job when her time is up?" Swinton shot back. Before the warden could respond, Swinton snapped: "You'd be a damn fool if you did. Don't you know she doesn't believe in prisons? Sure as you live, she'd let them all escape, and what would become of you then?"

If nothing else, Swinton's visit assured Goldman that nothing terrible would happen to her during the rest of her prison stay. Overnight the warden and the head matron extended privileges to Swinton's "little girl." Coffee, fruit, food from the warden's table, and walks around the prison grounds were suddenly hers. Goldman declined the extra rations. So long as the other inmates did not receive similar favors, she would not accept them either. But the chance to "inhale the spring air without iron bars" was more than she could resist.

Prison taught Goldman much. Up to that point in her life, Blackwell's Island was the "best school" she had ever experienced. In her hospital work, she acquired new skills and honed others. The warden's behavior taught her that even the powerful were not beyond manipulation. The inmates' response confirmed her experiences outside of prison: Ministering to the lowly required kindness without condescension. The John Swintons in her life gave Goldman a "new faith in the possibilities of America." That he was not an anarchist helped her realize that she did have friends and allies outside the movement. That he was a reformer convinced her that Americans, "once aroused, were as capable of idealism and sacrifice as my Russian heroes and heroines." Finally, prison gave her greater awareness of the "strength in my own being, the strength . . . [to] fight for my ideals."

Goldman was released from Blackwell's Island in August 1894. The depression that had begun the summer before had not lessened its grip on the nation. By late summer, perhaps one of every five wage earners was unemployed. As a result, efforts to rally the jobless, the unorganized, and the powerless had intensified. There were strikes and threats of strikes, demonstrations and rumors of demonstrations. In the weeks just preceding Goldman's release a march on Washington organized to demand publicly financed work relief and a national strike against the Pullman company both ended in utter failure and stunning violence. Federal troops deployed to crush the strike killed some thirty-seven people.

These events added to Goldman's determination to take her message directly to the American masses. More than ever, she was convinced that her mission was to work among the "natives" rather than the immigrants. From this point on, she vowed, she would devote herself to "propaganda in English," because "real social changes could be accomplished only by the natives." Ten months of confinement in a U.S. jail had not slowed the process of converting Goldman into an American radical.

First was a round of receptions and meetings her anarchist friends had organized. Most noteworthy was a gathering at Justus Schwab's saloon, where every New York radical of any reputation put in an appearance. Shocking though it was to some onlookers, men and women gathered together in the same drinking establishment. More shocking still, they entered the saloon by the same door. Once inside they were surrounded by more books than bottles. In the midst of all the hubbub was Schwab himself, the man who years earlier had invited Most to America, and a proprietor more interested in dispensing ideas than drinks.

Goldman relished this attention and despised it. Her memoirs refer to these days and weeks following her release as a perpetual "nightmare." A part of her wanted to be alone to reflect on her time in prison, and yet she savored the attention and the affection—and the prospect of a successful return to the podium that both promised.

The crush of admirers aside, Goldman was anxious to see a particular man and a particular woman. The man was Ed Brady, whom she had met in 1893 while both were working for the commutation of Berkman's sentence. The woman was Voltairine de Cleyre, a young anarchist who had been among her prison visitors.

Brady was a vagabond Irishman who years earlier had found his way to Vienna and the Austrian anarchist movement. There he served a ten-year jail term for publishing and distributing anarchist literature. Not long after his release he, like Most before him, migrated to America and to New York anarchist circles, where he found a home and where not long after Berkman's conviction a despairing Goldman found him.

Ironically, in Goldman's efforts to gain Berkman's release, she met a man who at least temporarily replaced Berkman in her life. Berkman was an activist, a revolutionary, and Goldman loved him for his commitment to the cause. But to Goldman he was one-dimensional. Brady, however, was the "most scholarly man" she had ever encountered. He knew not only politics and economics, but literature and philosophy. He introduced her to Shakespeare, Goethe, Rousseau, and Voltaire. More than that, he knew how to live the good life cheaply. He escorted her to Schwab's saloon and its eclectic collection of French, German, Italian, Spanish, Russian, and even American radicals. He improved her culinary skills by teaching her the intricacies of French cooking. And sometime during the first half of 1893 Ed Brady and Emma Goldman became lovers. For several stormy years they continued to be lovers. Prison intervened, arguments erupted, Europe beckoned, but their relationship survived longer than either had imagined it might in 1893.

In Brady, Goldman found a tender Most, a refined Berkman, and an attentive Kersner. She soon learned, however, that she had joined her life with that of another immigrant radical who had traditional notions about women and lovers. Like Most, Brady was looking for a wife to bear his children. He believed that every woman's destiny was motherhood and that Goldman's involvement with anarchism was both a denial of her natural instinct and a vain search for "glory and the limelight."

When her relationship with Brady began, Goldman was twenty-four, old enough, he decided, for her to be a wife and mother. But Goldman had already made up her mind not to have children. Years earlier she had rejected the surgery required to correct an inverted uterus and permit her to bear children. Recalling her own unhappy childhood, she felt no wish to add to the list of the world's "unfortunate victims"; therefore, she chose to cut herself off from motherhood at a time when women were discouraged from having both a career and children. In her memoir Goldman dwelt at some length on the "price" she paid for a childless life. It was not too high, she concluded, for in anarchism she had found "an outlet for my mother-need in the love of *all* children."

Though Brady never accepted her decision, he was there to renew his love on her release from prison. However, both knew that it was impossible to return to their life as it had been before Blackwell's Island. Brady had not rid himself of his desire to possess her, and Goldman now more than ever wanted to establish herself as a public personality. Complicating everything was her unending need for money, her renewed interest in a medical career, and the possibility of a female rival within anarchist circles.

Voltairine de Cleyre, according to Goldman, was the "poet rebel, the greatest woman anarchist in America." Born in upper Michigan in 1869 to a French socialist father who had fought in the Civil War and to an American mother with familial ties to abolitionism, de Cleyre came to anarchism through her family background and the free thought movement. Raised a Catholic and educated in a strict Canadian convent, she emerged from her adolescent years determined to liberate herself from all religion. That endeavor led directly to a commitment to helping others similarly inclined.

In 1887 de Cleyre became a socialist when she heard a young radical lawyer named Clarence Darrow lecture on the plight of the American working class. But socialism, for de Cleyre, was no more than a brief halfway house on her road to anarchism. Before long she was reading Benjamin Tucker and writing her own anarchist essays. Defining her societal goal as "liberty unrestricted by man-made law," she argued that "all forms of government rest on violence" and insisted that all Americans ought to live self-sufficient lives divorced from commercialism.

In 1889 de Cleyre moved to Philadelphia to live and work among the Jewish immigrants of that city. There, a century after the constitutional consolidation of the American revolution, she expected to find the "movers of the social revolution." Instead she met Goldman when the latter came to the City of Brotherly Love to speak in August 1893. At the time de Cleyre was ill, but she roused herself to attend the rally. However, before Goldman could address her followers, she was arrested at the request of New York police for her already infamous Union Square address. Fever or not, de Cleyre took Goldman's place on the platform in time to deliver a stinging attack against those who suppressed freedom of speech by arresting anyone who exercised that constitutionally ordained right.

Goldman was impressed then—and later: "I was proud of her comradeship."

Ironically, as the 1890s unfolded, Goldman and de Cleyre moved in opposite directions. An American native, de Cleyre looked to Jewish immigrants to restore the lost world of Thomas Jefferson. Goldman, on the other hand, was a Jewish immigrant who had cast her lot with American natives. Together, if separately, they were determined to bring about an American renewal and an anarchist future.

The next time these two fresh comrades saw one another was in December, when de Cleyre traveled to New York City to protest Goldman's conviction and to visit her on Blackwell's Island. In her speech, she compared Goldman to Jesus Christ and her judge to Pontius Pilate. De Cleyre went on to condemn the "hypocrites, extortionists, doers of iniquity, robbers of the poor, serpents and vipers" who had made a sham of the American legal system. Courts could not guarantee justice in America. Only the spirit of rebellion "will emancipate the slave from his slavery, the tyrant from his tyranny—the spirit which is willing to dare and suffer." Then, with Brady at her side, she paid a visit to one of the most spirited of rebels who then happened to be confined to Blackwell's Island.

Goldman thought this was the beginning of a "fine friendship." For years she had longed to have a close woman friend, a "kindred spirit" with whom she could share her "inmost thoughts". Instead of friendship, however, she encountered "petty envy and jealousy" from the men in de Cleyre's life. One of them, known only as A. Gordon, contributed directly to the dissolution of this "fine friendship." De Cleyre's lover and Most's disciple, Gordon once labeled Goldman a "disrupter of the movement" and charged that she aligned herself with anarchism "only for sensational ends." Therefore, when de Cleyre subsequently proposed that both she and Gordon visit Goldman in jail, Goldman informed her that she preferred not to see her friend, claiming that a "free woman" should not "expect her friends to accept her lover."

De Cleyre was offended. No more letters traveled between the two during Goldman's remaining months in prison. There were no more visits. In October 1894 de Cleyre was in New

York City to lecture. Goldman, then barely out of prison, was in the audience, but the two women did not speak. A promising friendship had fast developed into a very unfriendly personal rivalry.

Aside from their commitment to anarchism, the two women had little in common. Goldman was primarily an orator; de Cleyre was essentially a writer. Goldman loved public attention; de Cleyre could be a virtual recluse. Goldman earned her living from the podium; de Cleyre considered it immoral to take money while speaking out for anarchism. Each criticized the other's way of life. De Cleyre thought Goldman was too interested in the material distractions of the world. Goldman thought de Cleyre was too ascetic, too divorced from the real world, both materially and intellectually. Finally, each disdained the other's choices in men, and neither could keep her opinions on this sensitive subject to herself.

After 1894 Voltairine de Cleyre and Emma Goldman struck out on separate paths. Although neither ever surrendered her anarchist beliefs, their two paths never again became one.

At Brady's urging Goldman's path took her to Austria in the summer of 1895. Her months in prison had rekindled her interest in a professional medical career. Her year out of prison had convinced her that she could not survive financially on her speaking fees alone. Lacking the credentials, the money, and the time, she knew that becoming a physician was out of the question. That left nursing or midwifery. Brady told her that she could study both at the Allgemeines Krankenhaus in Vienna. Internationally known for its training of midwives, the institution offered a nursing degree as well.

Traveling with a passport under the name of Mrs. E. Brady, Goldman left for Austria in July via the British Isles. There she caused a minor sensation with her lectures on the sorry state of American political justice and the condition of the American working class. She also took time to make a pilgrimage to her "great teacher," Peter Kropotkin, who spent his days working in his carpentry shop and his evenings reading and writing. Goldman left their brief meeting convinced that "true greatness" in a person was invariably the result of living a simple life.

Goldman may well have believed in the virtues of living simply, but the quiet life was never to be hers—not in New York City, not in London, and not in Vienna. At the Allgemeines Krankenhaus she studied not only midwifery and nursing, but also the nature and treatment of childhood diseases. In what little spare time she had, she read Nietzsche, attended lectures by Freud, and visited theaters and concert halls.

Goldman returned to New York City in November 1896, armed with two degrees and anxious to work as a midwife. She was also willing to return to the apartment she had shared with Brady. Her hope was that they might renew their life together and spread the anarchist gospel. They might even work again on securing Berkman's release. She would surely concentrate on her return to the American lecture circuit. For the next few years, Goldman lived a very complicated life in simultaneous pursuit of old careers and new, old loves and new. Between exhausting days working among the immigrant women of the Lower East Side and Brady's incessant demands that she devote her life to him, she traveled as far west as Detroit and Chicago during 1897. The next year took her all the way to Los Angeles and San Francisco on the first crosscountry tour ever undertaken by an anarchist.

As she approached thirty, Goldman, on the platform, was on her way to acquiring a national reputation. The press was beginning to take note of her "sledgehammer" style. An anarchist comrade thought that the "secret of her power" resided in the "fact that she is the very embodiment of the doctrine she preaches." Her listeners took strength and energy from her—and gave both back to her. Her "lectures" were charged exchanges of the most elemental sort. Her audiences were not there simply to listen; they were there to shout encouragement, to throw out challenging or leading questions, to bait and heckle her. Seldom would she deliver a fully prepared lecture without interruption. Seldom would she be far into her speech before her remarks turned into an open dialogue.

The intensity of her convictions and the energy she generated in others were not Goldman's only virtues as a speaker. Sarcasm and humor were also staples of her performances. Beyond matters of technique, she thought of herself as an independent force, a sort of "free lance," ready to spread her ideas and to promote any local issue, any particular reform, any private organization she deemed worth of her support. Never would she allow herself to be tied to a cause that might detract from *the* cause. All the while preaching her increasingly individualistic brand of anarchism, she continued to work with feminist groups and labor unions without identifying herself as a feminist or a union woman.

National issues drew Goldman's attention as well. When William Jennings Bryan stumped the country for free silver in 1896 and after, Goldman condemned those "American liberals" who had fallen for this "new scheme." To her, politicians and political machines remained irrelevant to the search for "fundamental changes" in American society; Bryan in particular was a reform politician who struck her as "weak, superficial, and lack[ing] in sincerity." No politicians, not even the socialist Eugene Debs, deserved her full support. Only when she could be convinced that he was at heart an anarchist, that his socialism was "only a stepping-stone to the ultimate ideal," could she bring herself to praise him.

When Congress declared war against Spain in April 1898, Goldman declared verbal war on the United States. That politicians, such as Bryan, did not join her only confirmed her poor opinion of them. Conversely, she had "profound sympathy" for the "victims of Spanish atrocities" in Cuba and the Philippines. In fact, she worked briefly with members of the Cuban Junto in New York City. The answer to their plight, however, was not the presence of the U.S. army in either Cuba or the Philippines. Individual Americans might be motivated by feelings of humanitarianism, but the U.S. government was "not a disinterested and noble agency." Rather, the government and American capitalists had their eyes on cheap sugar and quick profits.

In 1898, Goldman's eyes did not stay focused on the presumed evils of an impending American empire. Too many evils within America needed to be eradicated first, and too many Americans had yet to hear her message.

Despite continuing pressures from Brady, Goldman continued to speak and to refine her message. She made clear her opposition to all forms of government, whether or not they were democratically elected. Elections, she contended, only gave people the illusion that they were involved in political decision making. Rather than political action, she advocated "direct action," by which she meant strikes and street demonstrations. Did "direct action" include assassinations? Here Red Emma (which in her younger days referred to the color of her hair, not her radical views) could be vague, but humorous. The "killing of rulers," she judged, depended on the position of the ruler. Russian czars should be dispatched immediately, but "if the ruler is as ineffectual as an American president, it is hardly worth the effort."

Goldman grew less reluctant to challenge socialist and populist calls for "statist" welfare programs and the nationalization of major industries. In addition, she became more outspoken in her criticism of organized religion. She told a congregation in Detroit that she did "not believe in God, because I believe in Man. Whatever his mistakes, Man has for thousands of years past been working to undo the botched job your God has made." When the subject turned to religion, she seemed to take an almost obsessive delight in scandalizing her listeners, either by asserting that Christianity was a religion "admirably suited to the training of slaves" or by denying that morality and religion had anything in common.

From the platform Goldman grew increasingly strident in her denunciations of conventional sexual morality. Issues of libertarianism were already competing with more collectivist economic schemes for her time and attention. In a lecture simply entitled "Vice," she argued that no sexual act, so long as it was entered into voluntarily, could be classified as a vice. An avowed and active heterosexual, her defense of sexual voluntarism extended to a defense of homosexuality and masturbation, both of which she contended should be approached from a scientific, rather than moral, standpoint.

All sexual repression was by Goldman's definition harmful, both because repression was physically and mentally unhealthy and because it inhibited the creative life. By the end of the 1890s, Goldman was using the phrase "free love" rather freely. In fact, another of her public lectures was shockingly titled "Free Love." In it, she defended sexual activity practiced by "varietists." The problem was that historically "varietism" had been the exclusive province of men. Women deserved equality in this sphere of life as well. To Goldman, the "sex question" of the late 1890s was essentially a woman's question. Women had to be free sexually if they were to be fully emancipated. Free women were crucial to the ultimate success of American anarchism.

Goldman herself practiced serial monogamy. "Free love" did not mean indiscriminate sexual activity; it meant love without a legal marriage, which she saw as little more than another form of prostitution. In her view the only form of marriage worth entering into was a "marriage of affection." Two people ought to live or love together only so long as "love exists" and no longer. In that regard, Goldman practiced exactly what she preached.

The more Goldman read (particularly of Nietzsche) and the older she got, the less convinced she was that personal happiness could be achieved through communal living or that mass action could bring about social change. More American individualist than European anarchist, Goldman was moving away from Kropotkin, who believed that all individuals, even the superior ones, drew their energy and inspiration from the masses. Goldman, self-proclaimed leader of the masses, was increasingly convinced that she was dispensing a lot more energy and inspiration to the masses than she was receiving from them. The masses, even those who attended her lectures, were too "ignorant" to give her much of anything.

If Goldman was increasingly disdainful of the masses in the abstract, she was also publicly critical of the American notion of "rugged individualism," which she associated with the excesses of Gilded Age capitalism. On the stump she was a rugged individualist. Without the aid of others, she had made herself into a leader, albeit a leader without a mass following. To secure that following, she no longer relied on Most's coaching, Berkman's bravado, or Brady's intellectualism.

In early 1899, Goldman and Brady came to a final parting. They had briefly separated many times before. The issue was always the same: Brady yearned for a wife, while Goldman did not want the encumbrance of a husband. This long-standing difference erupted into a crisis when Brady took an overdose of morphine. A shocked Goldman assumed that he had tried to kill himself, but his recuperation was proceeding so well that she was always hesitant to "dig up the ghastly affair." Days stretched into weeks without mention of his act. Then suddenly he surprised Goldman by informing her that he had never intended to take his life. He knew that he could stand a good dose of morphine, so he decided to swallow just enough to "scare you a little and cure you of your mania for meetings."

The shock of Brady's revelation was, to Goldman, at least as great as, if not greater than, the horror of the "suicide" attempt. Shock quickly turned to anger. "Mania for meetings?" That was his commentary on her career, on the entirety of her public life? Goldman did not know which loomed larger—contempt for his cowardice or fury over his refusal to understand her commitment to her cause. She only knew that this was the end of their seven years together.

And yet, as the 19th century drew to a close, a thirty-year-old Goldman was not really certain that she wanted so public a career after all. Between her speaking engagements, she still made time for a private life. Important work, meaningful work remained for her as an anonymous nurse among New York City's immigrant poor. She made long-delayed trips to Rochester to visit her family and to reconcile with her aging father. There were moments when she wanted nothing more than to have Berkman out of prison and by her side.

In 1899, Goldman returned to Europe, ostensibly to study medicine in Zurich. For a brief time a Czech anarchist named Hippolyte Havel became the love interest in her life. Together they helped plan an anarchist congress in Paris. While there, they managed to squander the money that Goldman's American benefactors had intended for her medical studies. Their funds exhausted, they hired themselves out as guides for American tourists in Paris, earning enough to pay for an inspection of the London slums en route to New York City in December 1900.

In the months that followed, Goldman contemplated another whirlwind lecture tour, when not wondering whether she should settle in with her Czech lover and minister to the city's burgeoning immigrant population. While suspended between two lives, she continued to be a subject of controversy. Attacks on anarchists, courtesy of the commercial New York press, focused on her. Condemnations of anarchist violence forced her to walk a tightrope between defending Berkman and endorsing his "deed." She seemed to enjoy the exchanges—and the attention—until another act of violence, this time in Buffalo, New York, made Goldman very much the center of national attention—and the focus of a nation's anger.

CHAPTER FIVE

Czolgosz . . . and After

❖
❖

On Friday, September 6, 1901, two Americans were on tour in cities far removed from one another. Their paths had never crossed – and for good reason. One was a solid Republican; the other was not. One had standing as a national leader; the other denied the legitimacy of any leader. William McKinley and Emma Goldman – the President of the United States and an anarchist who had contempt for both the office and the procedures necessary to obtain it. On that hot September day an unlikely event brought their lives together, even as it brought the life of one of them to an end.

That very afternoon President McKinley was visiting the Pan-American Exposition in Buffalo, New York. Between stops at the Tower of Light, studded with some 35,000 incandescent bulbs, and the Fountain of Abundance, he was scheduled to hold a ten-minute public reception. The site was the exposition's Temple of Music, normally used for recitals, but also equipped to handle ceremonial appearances. On this occasion the president was to give a brief speech and shake a few hands before leaving for Cleveland to attend a reunion of Civil War veterans.

Standing in the line of presidential greeters was a slender young man with slightly rounded shoulders, fine, wavy hair, and blue eyes, whose fixed stare gave him an empty, almost expressionless look. Dressed neatly in a striped gray suit, he drew no suspicious stares from the soldiers and Secret Service men assigned to guard the president. On this oppressively humid afternoon not even the handkerchief wrapped around his right hand occasioned a second glance. Hidden within the bandage was a loaded .32 caliber revolver with an owl's head stamped on either side of its handle.

At precisely 4:07 p.m., the young man had finally snaked his way to the head of the line. When he reached the president, McKinley instinctively offered to shake his left hand, thinking that the poor fellow's right hand was injured. Before their hands could join, the young man fired two shots from the revolver concealed within the bandage. One bullet struck the president in the breastbone, and the second tore into the left side of his stomach. Before lapsing into shock, the mortally wounded president could only plead, "Be easy with him, boys." Eight days later McKinley was dead and Theodore Roosevelt was president. For the third time within forty years an assassin's bullet had felled an American president.

Within seconds of the shooting, the assassin was clubbed to the floor and arrested. His name was Leon Czolgosz. When questioned as to why he had attempted to murder the president, Czolgosz shrugged, then deadpanned, "I done my duty." Whose "duty" had he done? His own? Silence. Was he carrying out another's orders? More silence.

Then twenty-eight years old, Czolgosz was the fourth of eight children born to Polish immigrant parents. His father worked for the Detroit sewer system, while his mother took in washing until her death in 1885. Poorly educated, Czolgosz worked during much of his youth as his family moved from Detroit to northern Michigan to Pittsburgh. Uprooted once more at eighteen, he accompanied his family to Cleveland, where he spent several years working in a wire factory. There he earned roughly ten dollars a week; there he was caught up in a bitter strike. It was not long after the strike that he began to attend socialist meetings in the upstairs hall of a saloon his father owned. Seldom did he contribute to the discussions, content instead to read and listen.

In 1898, Czolgosz suffered a mental breakdown, quit his factory job, and drifted aimlessly from city to city. During this time he came to believe that he was obliged to kill the president. In July 1901 he rented a room in a boarding house near Buffalo. Two months later he purchased his owl's-head revolver for four dollars and fifty cents. The time had come to do his duty.

Despite evidence that his sense of duty suggested at least a hint of insanity, Czolgosz was declared to be mentally competent to stand trial. It took a jury thirty-four minutes to find him guilty as charged. On October 29, 1901, a scant seven weeks after firing the two fatal shots, Czolgosz was executed for the murder of William McKinley.

On the day McKinley was shot, Goldman happened to be in St. Louis to lecture, propagandize, and recruit for anarchism. She had had a busy first year of the new century. Between her speaking and her nursing careers, she had granted a series of public interviews in a vain attempt to define anarchism for a mass audience. The question that kept recurring was the one that would never quite go away: Did Goldman endorse violence or did she not? Again and again, she confused herself and her listeners. Quick to express her loyalty to Berkman, she also placed education at the top of her list of approved anarchist strategies. As a result, she excused acts of violence without openly sanctioning them. On occasion, she would dismiss assassins as "utter fools." If pressed by reporters, however, Goldman could not bring herself to condemn any individual who ultimately resorted to such an act. She might argue with her "utter fool," but further than that she refused to go.

Goldman's travels continued to Chicago, to Cleveland, to St. Louis, and to numerous other cities across the country. In Chicago she had established close ties with local anarchists, including Abe and Mary Izaak, Russian Mennonites who had become anarchists sometime during the 1890s. While in California, they founded an anarchist magazine called *Free Society*, which Goldman admired because it placed sexual freedom on a par with all other liberties. The Izaaks subsequently moved to Chicago, where they hoped to find a larger readership for the magazine. With them, Goldman had both a second home and a second voice. In fact, for nearly three months in the spring and early summer of 1901, she lived and worked in Chicago with the Izaaks.

In May, Goldman left Chicago briefly to deliver one of her standard talks, "Modern Phases of Anarchy," to a meeting of the Franklin Liberal Club of Cleveland. In the audience was an inquisitive Leon Czolgosz, who seemed to be following a path trod by many youthful radicals of that era. Dissatisfied with socialism, he was drawn to anarchism—and to Goldman. During the intermission, in fact, he questioned her directly about additional books he might read on the subject.

If it was easy for Goldman to put one more aspirant to anarchism out of her mind, it was more difficult for her to ignore one of its longtime converts. Weeks after her trip to Cleveland, Goldman arrived in Rochester for a family visit only to find two letters from Berkman. On order of prison authorities, she had not communicated with Berkman for better than a year. Suddenly the rules had changed, and he was able to write. The first letter, dated July 10, left Goldman furious. In it, Berkman explained his silence. For a year he had been held in solitary confinement, including a period of eight consecutive days in a straitjacket. Near suicide and "rotting in my own excrement," he was released only when a new prison inspector intervened on his behalf.

The second letter, dated July 25, contained more encouraging news. A revised commutation law had reduced Berkman's sentence by two and a half years, leaving four years to serve in the penitentiary and a year in the workhouse. More than that, he could have visitors for the first time in nine years. That meant that he could see his "sister" once again. As soon as she could make arrangements, Goldman journeyed to Western Penitentiary, where she found a barely recognizable Berkman. "Thin and wan," he sat mutely with her for a few moments before an officious "time's up" interrupted their silent exchange. That shout, Goldman recalled years later, "almost froze my blood."

That same day, Goldman left for St. Louis, arriving there on September 5. The next day was to be filled with meetings and speeches, but her schedule was cut short. On her way to her evening appearance, she heard a newsboy call out: "Extra! Extra! President McKinley shot!"

Goldman was stunned, but no more so than anyone within earshot of the boy hawking papers. The next day, however, she caught a headline that contained a more discriminating shock. Screaming across the front page of a local newspaper was the following:

ASSASSIN OF PRESIDENT McKINLEY AN ANARCHIST.
CONFESSES TO HAVING BEEN INCITED BY EMMA
GOLDMAN. WOMAN ANARCHIST WANTED.

When Goldman first learned of the assassination attempt, her St. Louis friends warned her that efforts would be made to connect her to it. She refused to listen to "such a crazy story." She had "incited" no one to kill the president. Less than twenty-four hours after the two shots in the Temple of Music, however, she was forced to admit that these initial warnings had not been quite so ridiculous.

The next morning Goldman purchased several newspapers before sitting down in a local restaurant to sort out the details of the shooting and to ponder her response to the ominous headline. Alone, she read about a police raid on the Izaak household in Chicago. Nine people had been arrested, including the Izaaks, their son and daughter, and Hippolyte Havel. All had been charged with conspiring to kill the president, but only the senior Izaak's arrest had been requested by authorities in Buffalo. She also learned that some 200 detectives had already been dispatched to track down the notorious Emma Goldman! Then, on an inside page, she happened on a picture of the assassin, whom she recognized instantly. It was the young man who had first approached her in Cleveland a few months earlier. She did not know him as Leon Czolgosz but remembered him only as someone named Nieman, a surname he had adopted following the strike in the wire factory.

In early July, Nieman had mysteriously appeared at the Izaak home in Chicago. When Goldman answered the door, she recognized the "handsome chap of the golden hair" she had briefly visited with two months earlier. He was anxious to pursue a conversation, but she was literally on her way out the door, bound for the train depot and her family in Rochester. Undaunted, he rode with Goldman and Havel to the railway station, filling them in as they bumped along with tales of boring Cleveland socialists and with his eagerness to make contact with real anarchists.

Goldman listened attentively, but her thoughts were fixed on Rochester. She needed relief from the anarchist wars, and she was looking forward to seeing her sisters and their children, the first generation of her family born in America. When the three reached the station, she asked Havel to introduce Nieman to their circle of Chicago anarchists. Then she boarded her train, thinking no more about this, her second and last encounter with Czolgosz. Two months later she found herself sitting in a St. Louis restaurant, staring at a newspaper photo of McKinley's assassin, and thinking very hard about the shadowy Nieman, who was now known to the world as Leon Czolgosz.

If Goldman had easily dismissed Nieman from her crowded mind between July and September, her Chicago allies had not. Abe Izaak, for one, had been convinced all along that Nieman was a spy. So certain was he that he published a warning in *Free Society* on September 1. Calling his readers' attention to this enemy within their ranks, he described Nieman (without mentioning any names) as "well-dressed, of medium height, rather narrow-shouldered, blond, and about twenty-five years of age." Having already appeared at anarchist gatherings in Cleveland and Chicago, Nieman was forever "pretending to be greatly interested in the cause . . . or soliciting aid for acts of contemplated violence." Should he resurface anywhere else, *Free Society* readers ought to consider themselves "warned in advance." Goldman regarded such rumors as evidence of creeping paranoia among her anarchist allies. She liked Izaak, but when she read his caveat she was angry enough to write him demanding "convincing proof" of his charge. He had none, of course, but he insisted that Nieman was untrustworthy because he constantly talked about "acts of violence." In response, Goldman dismissed Izaak's suspicions as unworthy of anarchists, who ought to be welcoming converts rather than causing them to look elsewhere for an ideological home.

It was one thing for Goldman to question the legitimacy of another's fears. It was something else again to question the capacity—and the desire—of law enforcement officials to use the Czolgosz case to make her life very difficult indeed. Within a few days she not only tangled with Izaak over Nieman but waved off all friendly warnings to be on guard against a police dragnet. The newspapers strewn about her restaurant booth ought to have convinced her that the second threat was genuine: She was the subject of a nationwide hunt.

Goldman was far from the only anarchist to draw the attention of authorities—or pretenders to authority. In addition to the Chicago arrests, anarchist meetings were broken up in cities across the country. Some of this was police-inspired; the rest was the work of local vigilantes. In New York City, Most was arrested for reprinting a fifty-year-old German essay defending assassination as necessary for "historical progress." Most's mistake was to include it in the September 7 issue of *Die Freiheit,* which had been printed on September 5 and distributed hours before Czolgosz fired his fatal shots. When Most learned of the attempt on the president's life, he ordered the issue withdrawn from circulation. But it was too late. Copies had already been sold, and Most was arrested on September 12. For his poor timing he was tried, convicted, and sentenced to a year on Blackwell's Island.

Antianarchist sentiment was also prevalent in places across the country where anarchist communities had been established. From Tacoma, Washington, with its anarchist Home Colony, to the coal-mining town of Spring Valley, Illinois, with its growing number of Italian anarchists, to Guffey Hollow, Pennsylvania, with its perhaps twenty-five anarchist families, to Rochester, New York, home of Goldman and as many as one hundred other anarchists, police, press, and vigilantes shut down anarchist publications, drove anarchists out of town, and put others on trial on a myriad of trumped-up charges.

But Goldman was the anarchist atop everyone's most-wanted list. For nearly a decade she had been tweaking authority and getting away with it. Blackwell's Island had apparently taught her nothing. Moreover, in his signed confession Czolgosz had admitted that it was Goldman who had "set me on fire," that hearing her lecture had convinced him "to do something heroic for the cause that I loved." Officials in Buffalo were especially eager to find her in order to stage a trial that would convict both Czolgosz and Goldman for McKinley's assassination.

Goldman had no more finished reading her newspapers when "it became clear to me that I must immediately go to Chicago." The Izaaks and Havel were being held without bail. "It was plainly my duty to surrender myself." Duty? When she told an anarchist ally in St. Louis of her intention, he pleaded with her to change her mind. She was not persuaded. She knew that the police in Chicago and Buffalo had nothing to connect her to the shooting. True, she had met Czolgosz, but she certainly had not driven him to kill the president.

Despite the confidence she had in her defense, Goldman knew that the authorities were anxious to convict her of this crime. Given her well-advertised disdain for the U.S. legal system, she realized that formal proof was the least of the worries of her accusers. Nevertheless, she boarded the next train for Chicago.

Perhaps the memory of Haymarket was haunting Goldman once again. The ringleader of the Haymarket eight, Albert Parsons, had escaped the police dragnet after the fatal bomb had been thrown. For six weeks he remained in hiding in Wisconsin, where he worked in a bicycle shop until deciding he ought to stand trial with his comrades. He knew that he had done nothing wrong. Therefore, he chose to return to Chicago and establish his innocence.

Well aware of Parsons's ultimate execution, Goldman mulled over his fate. Perhaps she, too, sought martyrdom. Certainly she had her own flair for the dramatic. If the authorities wanted a trial, she would give them a trial. If her death was to be the result, what was that compared to the advance it might achieve for anarchism? So, thinking of both her moment on the witness stand and the converts to anarchism that her trial might generate, she was almost anxious to get to Chicago.

Goldman did not surrender instantly. Just before the train pulled into the station, she took off her glasses and put on a small sailor hat with a blue veil. While disembarking, she pulled the veil over her face before mingling among the patrons—several of whom "looked like detectives." Walking toward her contact, Goldman whispered brief instructions to delay their rendezvous until she could determine whether or not they were being followed. Only when she felt certain that the two had eluded police did she chance a meeting. Next they zigzagged their way across the city on a half dozen street cars before arriving at her contact's apartment. Goldman was finally in the heart of Chicago, but she was not yet ready to visit the Cook County jail. She was prepared to surrender, but only on her schedule and terms.

Her Chicago contact and his wife implored Goldman to leave the city as quickly as possible. More than that, they urged her to leave the country. Canada was their suggested destination. Otherwise, they warned, "it will be the same with Albert Parsons." That may well have been exactly what Goldman had in mind.

Having refused their offer to arrange passage to Canada, Goldman accepted temporary refuge from two wealthy Chicagoans, whom she identified only as Mr. and Mrs. N. Neither was an anarchist, but both admired her enough to risk taking her in, if only until she could orchestrate her own surrender. There had to be a public dimension to it, and Mr. N proved to be instrumental in arranging just that. He knew reporters from the Chicago *Tribune* and thought he could obtain $5,000 from the newspaper for an interview. He planned to bring a representative of the paper to their apartment as quickly as possible. Then the three of them would ride together to police headquarters, with Goldman granting the interview along the way.

Goldman liked the arrangement—the drama (for her ego), the publicity (for her cause), and the money (for her defense).

But the plan went awry. That evening the *Tribune* agreed to her terms. The next morning Mrs. N. left for work, Mr. N. went to fetch the waiting reporter, and Goldman waited in the apartment. After destroying any letters that could implicate her hosts, Goldman was prepared to spend the day alone until Mr. N. arrived with the reporter. If any callers happened by, she was to pretend to be the maid.

By 9 a.m. the "maid" had received more than her share of gentlemen callers—thirteen to be exact. They arrived at separate points of entry and in two shifts. Goldman discovered the first clutching the windowsill and shouting "Why the hell don't you open the door? Are you deaf?" With that he swung through the window, gun in hand. The startled maid had little time to think. She obeyed the command, at which point a dozen men swept into the room. The leader grabbed her by the arm and demanded her name. She recovered her composure just in time to be the maid: "I not speak English—Swedish servant girl." Apparently satisfied, the man released her, while the rest searched the apartment. Turning to the only woman in the room, he held up a photograph: "See this? We're looking for Emma Goldman. We want this woman. Where is she?"

This time the maid was no help at all. Pointing at the picture, she replied: "This woman I not see her. This woman big—you look in those small boxes will not find her—she too big." Frustrated, the intruders turned every room inside out without uncovering any evidence of their prey. Just as they were about to leave, one of the men suddenly happened upon a fountain pen with the name Emma Goldman engraved on it. Still not believing that he was in the presence of anyone other than a Scandinavian maid who spoke broken English, the captain mused that his quarry must have been there and might well return. Before taking his own leave, he ordered two of his men to remain behind. Just then Goldman decided that "the game was up." There was no Mr. N. and no *Tribune* reporter, so there was no purpose in maintaining the "farce" any longer. "I am Emma Goldman," announced the maid in unbroken English.

The date was September 10, four days after the assassination attempt and four days before McKinley's death. Escorted to police headquarters, Goldman was "grilled to exhaustion." At least fifty detectives took turns at shaking their fists in her face. A few actually struck her, but most simply threatened her if she refused to confess to being with Czolgosz in Buffalo. The huge captain was the "most ferocious" of the lot. Towering above her, he shouted menacingly, "If you don't confess, you'll go the way of those bastard Haymarket anarchists."

The next day Goldman was arraigned. Bail, however, was refused her, pending evidence from Buffalo authorities about her complicity in the assassination. In the meantime she was held in the Cook County jail without access to visitors or friendly letters. Hate letters she was given, unsigned letters that called her a "damn bitch of an anarchist . . . I wish I could get at you. I would tear your heart out and give it to my dog." Not until the third day of her incarceration did she receive word from a friend. Brady wired simply: "We stand by you to the last."

That same evening the chief of police paid a visit to Goldman's cell. Without any pretense of bullying, he asked her for a thorough account of her doings from her May exchange with Czolgosz to her September arrest. Goldman complied, save for any mention of her stop at Western Penitentiary. At the end of the interview the chief not only expressed his belief in her innocence but offered to leave her cell door unlocked. She could order her own food and newspapers. Mail and visitors could come and go as she—and they—pleased.

One of Goldman's first visitors was a lawyer from the Chicago office of Clarence Darrow, who was just beginning to establish a reputation as a defender of radicals and their causes. Goldman could not ascertain whether Darrow himself knew of his associate's visit, but she had no difficulty deciphering the message. Czolgosz was "crazy," intoned her uninvited guest. Therefore, it was in Goldman's interest to admit as much and sever all ties to him. If she continued to defend McKinley's assassin, "no prominent attorney" would be willing to defend her. Goldman was angry—angry at the lawyer and angry at Darrow, whom she had never met, for giving her "such reprehensible advice." That even those who purported to be sympathetic to anarchists expected her to "join the mad chorus howling" for the life of Czolgosz left Goldman more determined than ever to support him.

That same evening a reporter was amazed to hear Goldman tell him that in her "professional capacity" she would care for the dying President McKinley, even though her sympathies were with Czolgosz. "The boy in Buffalo" did what he did "for the good of the people," but a suffering McKinley was no longer an enemy. Near death, he was "merely a human being" in need of a kind and competent nurse. The next day this headline appeared in a Chicago paper:

EMMA GOLDMAN WANTS TO NURSE PRESIDENT;
SYMPATHIES ARE WITH SLAYER

That day McKinley died. Again reporters trooped to Goldman's jail cell, and again she surprised them. Was she sorry about the president's death? No. He was not the only person who had died that day. "Why do you expect me to feel more regret over the death of William McKinley than of the rest," many of whom had died "in poverty and destitution?" Goldman was not through: "My compassion has always been with the living; the dead no longer need it."

So far as Goldman was concerned, the country had gone crazy. There was panic in the air. There were calls for blood— Czolgosz's and Goldman's. But Goldman would neither confess nor abandon her "boy." She did not regard his act as irrational. After all, McKinley was a "willing tool of Wall Street and of the new American imperialism." His attitude toward labor was "reactionary" at best and "hostile" at worst. He had "repeatedly sided with the masters by sending troops into strike regions." All this weighed down on the "impressionable Leon, finally crystallizing in his act of violence."

Goldman did not abandon Czolgosz, before or after the Buffalo police gave up their chase for her. All during her stay in her Chicago cell the telegraph wires between the two cities were abuzz with negotiations over her fate. Finally, there was a formal court hearing before a Chicago judge. For two hours the verbal jousting between the Buffalo representative and the judge continued without interruption. The crux of the matter was obvious to everyone in the courtroom. Not a shred of evidence connected Goldman to McKinley's murder. The city of Buffalo had been denied its dual trial, and Goldman was once again a free woman—almost.

The date was September 23, and Goldman had been imprisoned for not quite two weeks. For better than half that time she had been held without bond. On September 18 bail had finally been set at $20,000 (separating her from the other eight anarchists, whose total bail was $15,000). Now she deserved her freedom and, she thought, an apology. Toward that end the mayor did concede that the only evidence against her in Chicago was that she was wanted in Buffalo. Nonetheless, she had to spend one more night in jail before finally obtaining her release.

On Goldman's first day of freedom, Czolgosz was convicted of McKinley's murder. Now Goldman resolved to give her full attention to Czolgosz's plight. From her cell she had kept herself informed of his shabby treatment. Neither family nor friends had been permitted to see him, and no attorney could be found to defend him. Consequently, the court assigned two lawyers to try his case. Both invested as much time in apologizing for their task as they did in performing it.

Buffalo anarchists had learned that, despite repeated beatings, Czolgosz had refused to sign a formal confession and had implicated no one else in the assassination. Few anarchists, however, in Buffalo or anywhere else, had been willing to work to assure him of a competent defense. As far as they were concerned, Czolgosz had done the movement great harm by shooting the president.

Although she was uncertain of Czolgosz's commitment to anarchism and unwilling to praise his deed, Goldman could not ignore Czolgosz the man. In fact, the more the press condemned him, the more outspoken Goldman grew in her support of him. Writing in *Free Society*, she described Czolgosz as a "supersensitive being . . . driven to some violent expression even at the sacrifice of his own life, because he [could not] supinely witness the misery and suffering of others." He was a "man with the beautiful soul of a child and the energy of a giant," a man "so pitiful in his loneliness and yet so sublime in his silence and superiority over his enemies." Then, in the same essay, she turned her fire on the "majority of anarchists" who had joined the "thoughtless rabble in its superficial denunciation of Leon Czolgosz." He deserved their sympathy, not their derision, for he, too, was a victim and a martyr, this "young man with a girlish face . . . pacing his cell, followed by cruel eyes."

In making her case, Goldman stood almost alone. Even Berkman, writing to her from his own prison cell, dismissed Czolgosz's deed as the act of an isolated individual, who had no grasp of social reality or the true needs of workers. To the man who had tried and failed to kill Henry Clay Frick, the McKinley assassination was an act of irresponsible terrorism. Goldman, deeply disappointed, knew that she was swimming against the current of anarchist thought. Too many of her compatriots had already decided that Kropotkin was correct: Legitimate social revolutions were engineered by the masses, not by a few individuals; mass resistance to oppression, not irrational acts of random violence, produced real social progress.

Goldman refused to accept this conclusion. She did stop short of endorsing political violence as sound anarchist strategy, but she also continued to argue that Czolgosz had done what he had done "for the people." More than that, she romanticized him as a hero of the people. As late as 1911 she insisted that those who engaged in such violence felt "intensely the indignity of our social wrongs." The villains were the "active and passive upholders of cruelty and injustice." Their greed—or indifference—ultimately forced her "saints" to act.

To Goldman, the combination of American "social and economic iniquities" and "sensitive souls" who could not tolerate such evils inevitably produced revolutionary violence. Given this tension, political violence was "similar to the terrors of the atmosphere, manifested in storms and lightning." Therefore,

those who resorted to violence were not guilty of criminal behavior; their actions were foreordained by the conditions that
surrounded them. By engaging in violence they became "modern martyrs," who welcomed death "with a smile" because they
believed, "as truly as Christ did, that their martyrdom will redeem humanity."

As of 1911, Czolgosz was, to Goldman, still "poor" Leon
Czolgosz. His crime consisted solely in having "too sensitive
a social consciousness." He was vastly better than his "ideal-
less and brainless American brothers," because his "ideals
soared above the belly and the bank account." Ten years after
the fact Goldman was still unable to rid herself of either her
anger at the "ignorant mass" or her romanticization of her
"boy."

Still, Goldman was careful to separate her movement from
her boy. Anarchism had not made him pick up a gun. It was
"utterly fallacious" to think that her philosophy was responsible for his act, or for any act of political violence for that matter. The "pressure of conditions" on a "sensitive nature," not
a philosophy that "values human life above things," caused
Czolgosz to arrange his rendezvous with the president.

Czolgosz may not have been an anarchist, and anarchism
may not have been grounded in violence. But he was still a
martyr and a saint for killing the President of the United States.
Moreover, he had succeeded where Berkman had failed. For
all his brilliance and commitment, Berkman had not killed
Frick, while Czolgosz had assassinated a president. Therefore,
by fighting for Czolgosz, Goldman was also fighting for
Berkman—and for herself. After all, while Goldman was innocent of any complicity in the McKinley murder, she had been
guilty of aiding Berkman in 1892. That Berkman himself had
repudiated Czolgosz's deed only made it more imperative that
she defend her "boy in Buffalo," if only because he had to pay
for his act with his life and neither she nor Berkman had had
to make that ultimate sacrifice.

For Goldman, the day of Czolgosz's execution was a day
of mourning in 1901 and for years afterward. Right to the end
the warden had attempted to draw a confession from him im-

plicating Goldman. Even as he was being strapped into the electric chair, he was asked, "Why do you shield that bad woman? She is not your friend. She has denounced you as a loafer. She said you begged money from her. Emma Goldman has betrayed you. Why should you shield her?"

From beneath his black mask, the condemned murderer muttered: "It doesn't matter what Emma Goldman said about me. She had nothing to do with my act. I did it alone. I did it for the American people." With that he died. From that date forward that "bad woman" could never forget October 29. As late as 1932 she confided to a friend that she did "not feel very cheerful," saddened as she was by the "memory of the treatment that poor boy received at the hands of the comrades." More than thirty years after the event, she attributed her lingering melancholy over Czolgosz's "treatment" not to the state that had executed him, but to her brother and sister anarchists, Berkman included, who had spurned him.

By 1901, Goldman had put a good deal of her immigrant anarchist past behind her. She had long since rejected Most. She had avoided much of the verbal warfare and the arcane ideological hairsplitting that went with being a radical. She had embraced American thinkers, American heroes, and the American language. She had started her search for converts to anarchism among the working class, and she had at least contemplated taking her case to the American middle class. She had even allowed herself the luxury of thinking that the American masses were not as ignorant and dull as she had long presumed them to be.

But always lurking just below the surface was the older Goldman, who was filled with romance at the prospect of revolution and violence in America and consumed with scorn for those too dense to appreciate either her voice or her sense of romantic revolutionary adventure. McKinley's assassination, as well as the subsequent persecutions of the obscure (Czolgosz) and the notorious (Goldman), at least momentarily revived the old Goldman. At the same time, she felt betrayed and depressed. After all, if not even Berkman understood her, what was the use?

The general reaction to McKinley's assassination and the resulting tendency of radicals to align themselves with socialists rather than anarchists gave Goldman additional reasons to wonder about the future of her ideal. In the aftermath of this assassination, socialism gradually became the dominant radical ideology in the United States. Moreover, technology and centralization seemed the wave of the future. Socialists, who had made their peace with the ballot box and the machine age, seemed poised to embrace that future. Anarchists, on the other hand, rejected centralizing schemes, whether bureaucratic or electoral, and questioned the connection between technology and progress. They placed the human spirit far above soulless machines. Nonetheless, it began to appear, even to radicals, that anarchism was a doomed, perhaps even reactionary doctrine out of tune with the 20th century.

To make matters worse, government agents continued to hound anarchists living in the United States, while the executive and legislative branches pressed for exclusion of immigrant-anarchists from U.S. shores. Ironically, just as anarchists began to decline in numbers and influence, demands for their removal and persecution increased. Overlooking the obvious fact that Czolgosz himself was native born, calls for legislation to keep anarchists out of the United States increased in the months following the assassination. In his first message to Congress, the new president, Theodore Roosevelt, declared war "not only against anarchists, but against all active and passive sympathizers with anarchists." Because anarchists and their apologists were "morally accessory to murder," he called on Congress to exclude from the country anarchists who advocated assassination and to deport aliens who espoused similar views.

Legislation toward that end began to work its way through both houses of Congress. Only conflicts between House and Senate bills prevented final passage in 1902. The House wanted to add to the list of unwelcome immigrants "persons who believe in or advocate the overthrow by force or violence of all governments, or of all forms of law, or the assassination of public officials." The Senate, on the other hand, wanted to exclude those who disbelieved in all government, as well as anyone affiliated with an organization teaching such views. Ultimately, Congress in March 1903 passed a bill closer to the Senate version. Roosevelt signed the legislation a day later.

By the time of the passage of the Anarchist Exclusion Act, Goldman had regained her enthusiasm for the fight. In the months following Czolgosz's execution, however, she could not bring herself to mount new platforms to make old arguments. Instead, she lost herself in the daily routine of a tenement nurse. For the time being she would not be the notorious Emma Goldman but an anonymous Miss E. G. Smith.

As 1901 drew to a close, Goldman found herself drawing on her own resources as she tried to make a new life for herself in New York City. She may have been at odds with Kropotkin over everything from the place of political violence in the coming revolution to the virtues of sex and city life in the unfolding present, but she thought she could still learn from her mentor. She could live a quiet, productive life working among the sick and the impoverished of New York City. Depressed as she was over the state of her movement, over attacks from without and divisions within, she hoped to be able to carve out a life apart from public anarchism. Miss E. G. Smith did not need the frustrations of the movement. Instead, the poor of the city needed her.

CHAPTER SIX

Mother Emma and Mother Earth

❖
❖

Goldman's retreat from the anarchist wars did not survive the year. By the summer of 1902 her yearnings for a public life were so strong that she would return to the platform before the year was out. Lecturing was not her only work in the first decade of the new century. In 1906, Goldman gave birth to her own magazine, appropriately named *Mother Earth*, which she nurtured through perpetually precarious times until its demise in 1917.

Also in 1906, Berkman was released from prison, having served fourteen years of his twenty-two-year sentence. Prison had neither reformed Berkman nor made him repentant. Instead, it had nearly destroyed him. The Berkman of 1906 was a broken man who desperately needed time and solitude so that he might piece his life together. He needed a mother more than a lover, and Goldman was there to minister to him, ever hopeful of playing both roles in his shattered life.

However, not long after their reunion, Goldman acquired a new love interest. In 1908, Ben Reitman, the "hobo doctor," entered her life. For the next several years Goldman was more deeply in love than she had ever been. But Reitman, too, seemed as much in need of a second mother as he was desirous of one more lover in his chaotic life. Goldman, of course, tried to be both.

Goldman could not live by Kropotkin's rules. Within her burned those "two fires." Kropotkin wanted his followers to be virtually asexual. Then anarchists really could lead less complicated lives. Goldman could neither be the former nor sustain the latter. One of those fires was easily kindled whenever Reitman was near.

To confuse matters further, the public Goldman vied with the private Goldman for control of her life. Whether she liked it or not, her name had become a national synonym for anarchism and anarchist-inspired violence. Thanks to an antagonistic press and her own refusal to abandon Czolgosz, Goldman personified the evil anarchist. No longer was she just another crank or one more harmless eccentric—she was a national menace. Both the Hearst and Pulitzer papers routinely labeled her a threat to all that was good in American values and institutions. To them, she was a "mischievous foreigner," a "wrinkled, ugly Russian woman," and still the mastermind behind the McKinley assassination. The *New York Times* also linked her repeatedly to Czolgosz, labeling her a radical divorced "from the mass of humanity" and a leader only for the impotent "army of the unwashed."

Ironically, the debate over the proposed legislation to exclude anarchists provided not only an occasion for Goldman's return to a more public life, but also a broader platform from which to speak. The McKinley assassination and her defense of the assassin had temporarily pushed Goldman to the fringes of the reform movement. But congressional reaction to the murder allowed her to renew contacts with nonanarchist reformers and radicals and to reestablish herself as a defender of something as American as the Bill of Rights.

So many progressives and radicals opposed the Anarchist Exclusion Act that Goldman took perverse satisfaction in their new awareness of the dangers posed by all political repression—even that targeted at anarchists. For her part, Goldman grew increasingly convinced that, given the tense postassassination atmosphere, anarchists could not afford to ignore potential allies. Progressives, socialists, and assorted ill-defined radicals surely did not agree with anarchists on all issues, but at least some among them could close ranks against narrow-minded legislation in favor of free speech. Hence her renewed interest in accepting speaking invitations from a great variety of reform organizations.

Not long after the passage of the Anarchist Exclusion Act, Goldman and her new allies had an opportunity to solidify their partnership and to test the new law. In October 1903 a Scottish anarchist and trade unionist named John Turner arrived in New York City at the invitation of American anarchists, Goldman included. A series of lectures had been arranged for him in advance of his visit, but only one was ever delivered. At the conclusion of that single lecture, Turner was arrested for having entered the United States in violation of the Anarchist Exclusion Act. No sooner was he arrested than Goldman took the podium to stem a threatened riot by those in the audience who wanted to rescue Turner forcibly from the police. As a result, he was taken into custody without incident.

Immediately following his arrest, Turner was searched. Found on him was a copy of *Free Society,* a Johann Most pamphlet, and a lecture schedule that included a memorial to the Haymarket anarchists. This was sufficient grounds for the U.S. Department of Commerce and Labor to order his deportation. A day later a federal court upheld this decision. The wheels of justice were grinding rapidly indeed.

With that, Goldman swung into action. Operating as Miss E. G. Smith so as not to antagonize the authorities or worry her followers, she visited Turner on Ellis Island, where he was being held pending deportation. Would he be willing to remain there while his case was appealed? she asked. At that moment Turner was locked in a nine-by-six foot cage reserved for any immigrant declared mentally incompetent. Despite his cramped quarters, he agreed to stay, not because he thought he would win a reprieve, but because he hoped that publicity surrounding his case would force repeal of the law under which he was being deported.

Goldman's next step was to organize a Free Speech League, whose membership included Benjamin Tucker as well as a number of prominent reformers who had no direct ties to anarchism. The League promptly engaged Clarence Darrow and his partner, Edgar Lee Masters, to represent Turner. They, in turn, decided to focus on the free speech ramifications of the case. "The sole question," according to the defense, was this: "Shall the federal government be a judge of beliefs and disbeliefs?" Tyranny, they warned, "always begins with the most unpopular man or class and extends by degrees; it should be resisted at the beginning."

The League's public campaign began with a Goldman-organized mass meeting in New York City's Cooper Union on December 3, 1903. Speaker after speaker rose to protest Turner's impending removal. In addition, similar meetings were held in other eastern cities and before various labor groups. In all, some two thousand dollars was raised for his defense, most of it a direct result of the efforts of one Miss E. G. Smith.

The crucial fight was before the Supreme Court. There Darrow and Masters pursued two lines of argument. First, they contended that Turner was simply a philosophical anarchist, who "regarded the absence of government as a remote political ideal." Second, they argued that the law itself was an unconstitutional limitation on the First Amendment guarantee of freedom of speech.

The Supreme Court disagreed. Writing for the majority, Chief Justice M. W. Fuller held that Congress had unrestricted power to exclude aliens, including "merely political philosophers," so long as Congress regarded their views as "so dangerous to the public weal that aliens who hold and advocate them would be undesirable additions to our population." Fuller went on to deny that coverage under the Bill of Rights extended to aliens seeking admission to the United States: "Those who are excluded cannot assert the rights in general . . . obtaining in a land to which they do not belong as citizens."

Obviously displeased by the verdict, Goldman was neither surprised by it nor sorry that she had helped to contest the original deportation decision. In her view, the fight was worth waging for the propaganda value alone. There were other, more personal, benefits as well. The battle for Turner's right to remain on U.S. soil also marked the full return of

Emma Goldman to the public arena. It was, however, a transition marred by doubts and second thoughts. "I never felt so weighed down," she confided to Berkman in January 1904, "so tired and worn out from and through people. . . . I feel as if I were in a swamp and try as much as I may I cannot get out . . . I fear I am forever doomed to remain public property and to have my life worn out through the care for the lives of others."

The call for freedom of speech was a convenient rallying point for those who expected to face attacks for swimming against the American mainstream. Therefore, it was in the interest of all such swimmers, anarchists or not, to establish their credentials as Americans by holding other citizens to the high standards set by the Bill of Rights. The problem was that civil liberties issues did not strike a popular chord among Americans generally at this time. Not until the repression following U.S. entry into World War I did civil libertarians organize specifically in defense of the Bill of Rights. In the midst of a war, their position could not be described as wildly popular.

Finally, if Goldman acquired new allies in her ongoing battle against the coercive state, she renewed old friendships at the same time. Kropotkin wrote to her following the Turner decision that the court's judgment was bitter proof that American society "throws its hypocritical liberties overboard, tears them to pieces—as soon as people use these liberties for fighting that cursed society." Goldman shared Kropotkin's cynical sentiments, but she was far from ready to cease fighting or to stop using "these liberties" in her efforts to remold America's "cursed society."

Money, however, was an issue Goldman had to address before concocting new ways of spreading her message or further testing the First Amendment. Earning a living was not an easy proposition for a professed anarchist. Goldman was more fortunate than most in that she did have another skill. But nursing, she was discovering, took too much time and energy from her primary calling. For a brief time, her solution was to open a legitimate massage parlor, advertising herself as a "Vienna Scalp and Facial Specialist." In addition, she became a combination press agent, interpreter, and manager for a visiting company of Russian actors. Their leader, Pavel Orleneff, wanted to bring the works of modern playwrights to working-class audiences. This adventure in "theater for the people" represented the kind of union between art and politics that Goldman had long advocated. With Orleneff, she began to explore the possibility of producing original plays, including a dramatization of Berkman's life, for a small theater that she hoped would become an "oasis in New York dramatic art."

All was going well until the collapse of the Russian Revolution of 1905, which opened the way for another round of Jewish pogroms all across Russia. According to Goldman, there were "hideous whispers" in New York that Orleneff's troupe contained "organized Russian Jew-baiters," prompting a Jewish boycott against his theater. The New York radical press sought to counteract both the rumors and the boycott, but to no avail. Unable to withstand this wave of bigotry, Orleneff's theater closed its doors for good.

Goldman, however, was not ready to surrender. Working without pay, she organized a tour of Orleneff's players in cities as far west as Chicago. As an impresario, Goldman was a moderate success, but she was not able to raise enough money for Orleneff to start anew and independently. Having once planned on spending many years in the United States, Orleneff decided that he had no alternative but to return to Russia. Before departing, he agreed to stage a benefit performance for Goldman, who was about to branch off into the publishing business. At various times over the years she had expressed an interest in starting a magazine. In the aftermath of the disappearance of Orleneff's "oasis," that wish began to take form. Her plan was to recruit idealistic writers who "breathe freely . . . in limited space." That "space" was tentatively to be called *The Open Road.* When the editor of a publication by the same name threatened suit, however, Goldman relented.

"Poor Walt Whitman," lamented Goldman, "would surely have turned in his grave if he knew that someone had dared to legalize the title of his great poem." Still, she had no choice but to "christen the child differently." What to name it? A few weeks before its anticipated birth on March 1, 1906, Goldman went on a weekend retreat to a small farm near Ossining, New York, where she observed that winter was releasing its hold on the earth, where specks of green revealed "life germinating in the womb of Mother Earth." That was it! Mother Earth was the perfect name for her child. After all, Mother Earth was the "nourisher of man, man freed and unhindered in his access to the free earth!" And Goldman had long claimed to be intent upon remaking the earth so that all people had an opportunity to be productive on it.

The next day Goldman returned to New York to conclude preparations for the first monthly issue. On March 1, *Mother Earth* appeared as promised, all sixty-four pages. For the next eleven years, Goldman would coax her child along. This was, after all, her forum for anarchism. But in its pages she would also offer support to those she had even temporary sympathy with. Meanwhile, her goals were to promote equality in economic dealings, freedom of artistic expression, and equality and freedom in sexual relations.

Finally, *Mother Earth* was to be a part of the "lyrical left" for whom songs of revolution were songs of personal liberation. For her part, Goldman never wanted to be trapped into thinking or believing that everything in life was reducible to grim, humorless economic terms. Nor did she want her magazine to ignore art, theater, and literature. The problem was that Goldman had difficulty thinking of these worlds apart from the role each played in promoting a revolutionary agenda, and that agenda inevitably meant repetitive propagandistic attacks on her capitalist enemies. As a result, at times she and *Mother Earth* could be mighty humorless in pursuit of their elusive revolution.

For the time being the birth of *Mother Earth* was an occasion for dancing and celebrating, for Goldman's consolidating her circle of anarchists, and for reaching outside that immediate group. The first issue included an essay outlining the fundamentals of anarchism, a diatribe against nationalism and

Zionism, a report on the arrest of Bill Haywood for the murder of the former governor of Idaho, a review of Henrik Ibsen's published letters, and a Goldman article titled the "Tragedy of Women's Emancipation." Art, politics, economics, and anarchism were one under the protective wing of Mother Emma.

In her contribution, Goldman set herself apart from orthodox feminists, whose "tragedy," in her view, resided in their limited understanding of emancipation. The right to vote, equal civil rights, and access to job opportunities might all be "good demands" in and of themselves, but none of them led to "true emancipation," which did not begin or end at the polls, in the courts, or on the job.

The time had come for each woman to "emancipate herself from emancipation, if she really desires to be free." With or without the vote, women will never reform politics. At the same time, "working girls" had only exchanged the "narrowness" of the home for the confinement of the factory, and the educated woman was a "professional automaton," whose "tragedy . . . does not lie in too many but in too few experiences." None was truly human, because none among them had confronted her interior self.

The source of the trouble was a "puritanical vision" that confined "emancipated women" either by stultifying their emotional lives or by banishing men entirely from their lives. All women needed to recognize that the "most vital right is the right to love and be loved." This meant dispensing with the "ridiculous notion that to be loved, to be sweetheart and mother, is synonymous with being a slave or subordinate." Each woman should take the time to listen to the "voice of her nature, whether it calls for life's greatest treasure, love of a man, or her most glorious privilege, the right to give birth to a child." Curiously, in this maiden issue, Goldman chose to attack both feminists who had rejected what she had embraced — namely men — and feminists who had spurned what she had spurned — namely motherhood.

Mother Earth was Goldman's child. On the second anniversary of its founding she referred to it as a "child . . . begotten by a great, intense love, the love for Freedom, for Human Justice. Those who gave birth to 'Mother Earth' were . . . united by love, by an ardent desire to rouse man from his stupor." Having seen her "infant" through its normal run of childhood "diseases," Goldman was ready to declare *Mother Earth* a "universal baby" no longer dependent solely on its parents. Besides, the "mother must forego the comforts of a home, exposing herself to many hardships while racing about the country, seeking new friends for her child." Forever claiming martyr status, this mother soon discovered that she had to leave home frequently so that her child might grow and thrive.

During these years, Goldman's home was an apartment at 210 East 13th Street in Greenwich Village. This address doubled as an editorial office for *Mother Earth* and a clearinghouse for the anarchist movement. Whether or not Goldman was actually there, the apartment was home to a workers' collective whose central task was to produce *Mother Earth*. Whether or not Goldman was directly involved with the collective, her life had a purpose for the first time in almost five years. With a small multitude of like-minded immigrant anarchists, she used her magazine to further an "American anarchist" movement by trying to appeal to the middle class and professional American reader, while at the same time reminding them that anarchism was alive and well in Europe. Even though Goldman was seldom a hands-on editor, *Mother Earth* had her mark on many more pages than its cover. It included reports on her speaking tours, essays written by her mentors (including Kropotkin), selections from her American heroes and heroines, and departments given over to poetry, short stories, and literary criticism. It included challenges to other radicals to avoid the dangers of centralization and cheers for those in the streets and fields organizing strikes and demonstrations. The magazine, in sum, sought to combine the philosophical and the practical, the American and the European, the stridently polemical and the daringly avant-garde.

Despite her literary pretensions, Goldman was a propagandist at heart. Modern artists (including Ernest Hemingway and D. H. Lawrence) and modern media (especially film) did not interest her. Moreover, Berkman, who had assumed the major share of the editorial duties by 1908, had been out of the flow of U.S. political and literary life for many, many years. If Goldman placed polemics ahead of art, Berkman ignored art altogether in his single-minded pursuit of the revolution. In one sense, he was the more honest of the two. While claiming an interest in art and literature for its own sake, Goldman invariably saw both as tools to advance her war on capitalism. Typical of her thinking was an essay titled "The Modern Drama: A Powerful Dissemination of Radical Thought," in which she praised literary figures who brought radical ideas to wider audiences. Goldman as literary critic could be quite provincial herself, however. The only literature really worth reading was literature that promoted "social discontent," thereby swelling the "powerful tide of unrest that sweeps onward and over the dam of ignorance, prejudice, and superstition." Berkman, on the other hand, simply dismissed all art as irrelevant to the life of the true revolutionary.

The date of Berkman's "resurrection" (Goldman's word) was May 18, 1906. On that day he boarded a train for Detroit, where a fellow anarchist-inmate was living and where he hoped to reacclimate himself to freedom far away from the pressures of New York City. Goldman had arranged a lecture tour so that she would be there to meet him. Not since her brief, silent visit with him just prior to the McKinley assassination had she seen him. And not since he had gone off to Pittsburgh to shoot Henry Clay Frick had she laid down beside him.

Within seconds of spying Berkman "swaying" toward her from his railroad car, Goldman's sincere excitement turned to anxious bewilderment. Berkman's face was "deathly white, [his] eyes covered with large ungainly glasses; his hat too big for him . . . he looked pathetic, forlorn." Gripped by "terror and pity," Goldman placed a bouquet of roses in his hand, then threw her arms around him and pressed her lips to his. Reminiscent of August 1901, nothing was said. Clinging to his arm, she walked with him out of the depot "in silence."

That night Goldman talked of "unessential things" until, "utterly exhausted," she dragged herself off to bed. Berkman, "shrinking within himself, lay down on the couch. The room was dark, [with] only the gleam of [his] cigarette now and then piercing the blackness." Goldman felt "stifled and chilled at the same time." Then Berkman came toward her and touched her "with trembling hands." For a long time they lay "pressed together" in silence. Suddenly, Berkman tried to speak. Before a word came out, he "checked himself, breathed heavily, and finally broke out in fierce sobs." When he gained control of himself he said only that the "walls were crushing" him, that he wanted to go for a walk. When he left the room and closed the door behind him, Goldman knew "with a terrible certainty" that the "struggle for Sasha's liberation had only begun."

That struggle continued at Ossining, where the two set up housekeeping. There Goldman hoped Berkman would finally begin to free himself from the "grip of the prison shadows." Instead, the "black phantoms of the past" continued to haunt him, driving him from the farmhouse, forcing him to roam the woods for hours, "silent and listless." The solitude, he confided to Goldman, was too much for him. He had to return to the city and the cause or he would "go mad."

After moving to Goldman's New York apartment, a distracted and exhausted Berkman was unable to find any suitable work. Her solution was a lecture tour. Perhaps a public unburdening of "phantoms" would bring back "his old faith in himself." In desultory fashion, he consented. He appeared in Albany and Syracuse, then Pittsburgh, even though Goldman "hated" the idea of his returning to that "dreadful city" so soon after his release. After all, according to the Pennsylvania commutation law, Berkman remained at the mercy of that state's authorities for eight more years. When a telegram arrived the day following his Pittsburgh meeting, Goldman was apprehensive. But all had gone well. The lecture had been a success, and the police had left Berkman alone.

Cleveland was the next—and unexpectedly last—stop. Following his opening lecture, Berkman left the house of his host and never returned. For three days his whereabouts remained a mystery. Then, just as mysteriously, he resurfaced at a New York City telegraph office from which he finally sent word to Goldman. This reunion was a carbon copy of the previous one: an ecstatic, emotional Goldman met a silent, sullen Berkman.

After dinner, a bath, and a concoction of whiskey and hot broth, Berkman talked. He had hated the idea of a speaking tour from the moment Goldman had suggested it. Just thinking about his next lecture was enough to throw him into a panic. But he kept on until Cleveland, where the talk was poorly attended and the ride to his host's farm interminable. That night he awoke from a heavy sleep to find a strange man snoring by his side. Prison had converted "close human proximity" into sheer "torture." Instantly he ran from the house in search of solitude. But being alone, he discovered, was not enough. He could escape other people, but he could not escape the feeling that there was no longer any purpose to living. The next morning he walked back to Cleveland, and that afternoon he purchased a revolver.

Berkman's plan was to go to Buffalo, where he knew no one and where he could go unrecognized on the streets and unclaimed upon his death. After a day of roaming the city he failed to pull the trigger. Instead, he returned to New York, as if drawn by some "irresistible force." After two days of "constant terror," he walked into the telegraph office and sent his message to Goldman.

By reaching out to Goldman, Berkman had taken a step away from suicide. But not until weeks later was there any significant change in his behavior. In October, Goldman had joined friends protesting the arrest of anarchists who had gathered to commemorate the Czolgosz execution. For her efforts, she was also arrested. That lit a spark under Berkman. Upon learning of her incarceration, he decided to join the fight to secure everyone's release, declaring that his day of "resurrection" had finally come.

No prosecutions were forthcoming, but the police continued to raid anarchist meetings through the winter of 1906–1907. Even a harmless masked ball to raise money for

Mother Earth was deemed a sufficient enough threat to produce fifty police officers to crash the event, unmask the revelers, and close the hall. No one was arrested, but the lost revenue was a blow.

A year after its birth, *Mother Earth* was still struggling for life. Its dollar-a-year subscription list had barely reached 2,000. The newsstand price of ten cents a copy ought to have been low enough to attract a working-class readership, but few genuine workers bothered to sample it. Goldman, however, was still determined to breathe life into the magazine. Publishing it represented for her a union of means and ends. Therefore, if more capital was needed, she would strike out on longer, more elaborate tours to raise it.

This decision freed Goldman from editorial work, which she was essentially not interested in, leaving her "child" in the uncertain hands of Berkman. Following his near suicide, he lapsed into a state of aimlessness, interspersed with bouts of uncontrollable envy. The contrast between his dreamworld of 1892 and Goldman's active world of 1907 was finally too much for him. Having plunged "into the current of events," she was no longer his "little sailor girl." Instead, she was now a woman of nearly thirty-eight, a woman who had undergone "profound changes," a woman no longer willing to fit into his mold. He had become aware of these differences almost immediately after his release. During the ensuing months, envy ate away at him. Instead of coming to terms with the Emma Goldman of 1907, he grew increasingly "resentful, critical, and often condemnatory" of her, her views, and her friends.

Goldman's periodic reaction to Berkman's belligerence was to want him out of her life completely. She had responded to his erratic behavior with the kindness of a mother and a lover. But he had met every overture with a new charge of "revolutionary inconsistency" or renewed assertions of "intellectual aloofness." At the end of her patience, Goldman hit on her final solution: Berkman could assume editorial control of the magazine. Old anarchist friends—Hipployte Havel, Max Baginski, and even Voltaraine de Cleyre—would be there to assist him. More to the point, Goldman would not be there to help, or to hector. Long lecture tours were necessary to keep *Mother Earth* afloat. In the meantime, she offered him a chance to sink or swim on his own. By bringing him within the *Mother Earth* family, she had also acted to enmesh their two lives in a new way.

Under Berkman's editorial reign, *Mother Earth* did not acquire a saucy sense of humor, but it did gain new readers, perhaps as many as 10,000 annually before his tour of duty ended in 1915. Initially, Berkman seemed reluctant to take command of the magazine. He wanted to produce a weekly propaganda newspaper that would appeal exclusively to workers. To him, anarchism was the left wing of the labor movement, rather than a statement of personal liberation. Nonetheless, *Mother Earth* turned out to be an acceptable vehicle for him and his mission: to convert workers to his conception of revolutionary anarchism.

Berkman was prone to feelings of bitterness, but he no longer possessed any such feelings toward the American working class. When he entered prison he had been disdainful of those working-class prisoners who not only failed to understand why he had tried to kill Frick, but who openly condemned his attempt on the steel baron's life. However, by the time of his release those sentiments had left him. In addition, he had lost all enthusiasm for revolutionary assassinations. Something was wrong with the tactic itself, not with the workers who opposed it. As *Mother Earth* editor, his goal was to convince workers to look at their economic lives as a prelude to painstaking organization, rather than as a rationale for instant revolutionary violence.

On this point Berkman and Goldman remained at odds. While he sought to appeal to the minds of American workers, she still wanted to hook the emotions of the rising middle class. Curiously, that meant focusing on noneconomic issues and romanticizing individuals, including, at times, violent individuals.

Goldman still held out hope that she and Berkman would once again be lovers. While off lecturing for *Mother Earth*, she wrote letters to him expressing her desire to "get back to my darling lover who means life, joy, happiness to me." She wanted nothing more than to "nestle close to you and in your strong passionate embrace." But there would be no more passionate embraces between the two. Now they would only be comrades—and sometimes uneasy ones at that. His envy did not fade away quickly, and her frequent absences did not help matters. One result may have been a trunkful of rather one-sided love letters; but another outcome was a love affair between Berkman and a fifteen-year-old New York anarchist named Becky Edolsohn. For the first, but far from the only time in her life, Goldman experienced what it was like to be the spurned older woman.

In her memoirs, Goldman rationalized Berkman's behavior, while simultaneously belittling him and elevating herself: "Sasha was two years younger than I . . . but he had not lived for fourteen years, and in regard to women he had remained as young and naive as he had been at twenty-one. It was natural that he should be attracted to Becky rather than to a woman of thirty-eight who had lived more intensely and variedly than other women double her age."

Wounded by Berkman's rejection, Goldman gradually accepted Edolsohn into her *Mother Earth* clan and eventually adopted the sole role of self-designated mother in Berkman's life. Not long after learning of the romance, Goldman left New York City for an anarchist congress in Amsterdam. For the first time in more than ten years, anarchists and pretenders to anarchism from around the world gathered to debate the meaning of their philosophy and to chart a course for its future. One of the key issues was the relationship between anarchists and syndicalist unions, which were based on the idea that working people could gain control of government and industry if they were willing to resort to highly disciplined general strikes and even selective sabotage. Goldman sided with anarchist delegates who feared a loss of anarchist identity if they joined forces with this brand of revolutionary unionism. Furthermore, she worried that anarchism would become nothing more than a working-class movement, if the syndicalists among them predominated. Still confused as to which was primary—the individual or the community—Goldman argued that "individual autonomy" was the essence of anarchism, while at the same time holding out for the possibility of spontaneous mass insurrections (as opposed to organized general strikes). To her, organization did "not foster individual freedom," but spelled the "decay of individuality."

The congress ended without a clear winner between anarchists and syndicalists, or without any discussion of women's issues by Goldman. Curiously, her defense of individualism did not lead her to so much as suggest that women had unique problems that anarchists ought to address separately and thoroughly. In fact, as she neared forty, Goldman was facing one of those problems herself: how to live a fulfilled life as an independent woman. Despite a public persona of strength and forcefulness, she was beset by inner doubts. Despite an apparently full life, there remained a "void" that she was reluctant to confront but from which she could not escape. Was she referring to herself when she discussed the "tragedy of women's emancipation"? Did she believe that her most "vital right" was the "right to love and be loved"?

At times, Goldman tried to fill her void by resorting to her version of motherhood. Whether producing a child in *Mother Earth* or attempting to mother her former lover into loving her once again, Goldman could be preoccupied with her need to exercise that "most vital" of rights. Having released *Mother Earth* and Berkman to live lives of their own, she had to wonder what, or who, would fill that void, what, or whom, she would love next. And would she ever be able to express that love without smothering its object?

The answer to the first question was not long in coming. In the spring of 1908, Goldman was on yet another speaking tour. Chicago had always been virtually a second American home for her. Next to New York City, it was the leading center for American anarchism. In Chicago in March 1908, Emma Goldman met the man who would cast a spell—and a pall—over her life for years thereafter.

The unlikely meeting between the two stemmed from Goldman's difficulty in finding a suitable lecture hall in the city. The "old trick of the police of terrorizing landlords" had made it nearly impossible for her to rent a hall. When she had almost given up hope of speaking in the city at all, Goldman learned that a young doctor who worked among the poor and unemployed was willing to convert a store he owned into a temporary lecture hall. At times the building was home to the doctor's Brotherhood Welfare Association, which provided social services and political organizers to the city's poor. Goldman knew little of his work, but she had heard of the doctor, because the local press had reported his role in a march of Chicago's unemployed. Now that he was offering her a place to speak in, she was doubly curious to meet him.

That sense of curiosity did not leave Goldman when the doctor arrived at her hotel room sporting a large black cowboy hat, a flowing silk tie, and an oversized cane. Goldman describes the rest of him as follows: "My visitor was a tall man with a finely shaped head, covered with a mass of black curly hair, which evidently had not been washed for some time. His eyes were brown, large and dreamy. His lips, disclosing beautiful teeth when he smiled, were full and passionate. He looked a handsome brute. His hands, narrow and white, exerted a peculiar fascination . . . I could not take my eyes off his hands. A strange charm seemed to emanate from them, caressing and stirring."

The doctor remained with her for several hours, discussing the details of her use of the store and the possibility of staging a concert in Workmen's Hall, where she would speak without any prior (police-attracting) public notice. When he left, Goldman remained "restless and disturbed, under the spell of the man's hands." That night she was unable to sleep. Why, she wondered over and over again, had she trusted him with the secret of the Workmen's Hall plan? She had "always opposed ready confidence in strangers." But this stranger held an "intense attraction" for her. Furthermore, she was quite aware that he had been "aroused" as well; "he had shown it in every look." So began Goldman's storm-filled love affair with twenty-nine-year-old Dr. Ben Reitman, known about Chicago as the Hobo Doctor. To Goldman he was simply Ben, or the Doctor. And what did Dr. Reitman call Goldman in his most tender moments? Mommy.

CHAPTER SEVEN

At Odds

The final decade of Goldman's life in the United States encompassed the years of her greatest notoriety, complicated by her continuing ambivalence toward nonanarchist reformers. As if the confusions of fame were not enough, these were also her years with Ben Reitman, the "Great Grand Passion" of her life. Along the way, she became *the* Emma Goldman—celebrity radical. This meant, among other things, that choices she had assumed were hers to make were often made for her. She could not simply retreat from the public eye when she wished to do so. For better or for worse, she was a public person no longer able to choose between her public and private worlds—and less able to maneuver between them.

Ironically, Goldman's altered status heightened the significance of the choices that remained hers to make. At various points between her tours and her deportation she was willing to support causes and individuals outside the anarchist fold. While still a spokeswoman for anarchism, she also lent her voice to the economically deprived working class and to the psychologically stifled middle class. Inclusion, not exclusion, was at the heart of this anarchist's approach to nonanarchist America. Inclusion did not mean, though, that she would permit anarchism to be relegated to a small corner in someone else's larger house. Hence, she was often at odds with other radicals, because she refused to sacrifice her anarchistic vision to other, more immediate, reforms. Other radicals, in turn, kept their distance from her, precisely because she would not renounce her anarchism.

Still, just as Goldman was taking on a public identity as the "High Priestess of Anarchism," she found herself enmeshed in the most compelling love affair of her life. Having established the "right to love and be loved" atop her private bill of rights, she thought she had finally found the man who would at once "love the woman in me" and "share my work." Never had one man been able to perform both roles. Ed Brady loved her, but he never understood her love for her work. Alexander Berkman loved her as well, but he loved Emma Goldman the anarchist more than he loved Emma Goldman the woman. Sharing their lives with one another was less important to him than sharing their work for the revolution.

In Ben Reitman, Goldman thought she had stumbled upon someone who embodied an abiding fervor for anarchism *and* for her. Born in 1879 to Jewish immigrant parents, Reitman grew up among the blacks and Irish of Chicago. Living with outcasts led him to entertain the notion of becoming one of them himself. After listening to hobo tales in the South Side railroad yards, he ran away from home for the first time at the age of eleven. At seventeen, he joined the army, only to desert within a few months. At eighteen, he tramped across the United States before returning to Chicago intent upon becoming a doctor for the downtrodden. At twenty-five, he began a professional lifetime of bringing medicine and preaching hygiene to the unwashed. But even after he had established his practice, Reitman could not resist the lure of the road. He was the Hobo Doctor not simply because he ministered to the homeless but because he sometimes was driven to return to his wanderlust ways.

No matter how far or often he roamed, Chicago was always home to the man who had set out to "rid the world of poverty." Having set so large a goal for himself, Reitman was never anxious to be pinned down to particulars. For that matter, neither was Goldman. If he had had difficulty choosing between a medical career and a life of social activism, so had she. Apart from the obvious physical attraction, that sense of suspension between two worlds was a part of his fascination for her. Here was both a "naive child" and a trained physician. Here was someone to mother and love. Here was a man who dreamed of saving the world, while working to cure a little corner of it in the interim. What was so wrong with that? Had not *the* Emma Goldman had the same dream? Had not nurse E. G. Smith operated similarly?

Ten years her junior, Reitman probably saw Goldman as a woman of strength and passion who might just bring a modicum of order to his otherwise chaotic life. He never remained in one place or at one task or with one woman for very long. Married, a father, and divorced before he was twenty-three, he behaved as though his version of saving the world demanded that all the women in it have the pleasure of his company, however briefly. In an unpublished autobiography, he justified his philandering by explaining that he was descended from a long line of "family deserters." Unfaithfulness was almost expected from a Reitman. He was unfaithful to the many women in his life, including the woman who wanted to love him and mother him without interference from potential rivals for either role.

Two obstacles stood in Goldman's way: Reitman himself, who was seldom satisfied with a single lover, and his biological mother, from whom he alternately could not and would not escape. Goldman sensed that she was asking for trouble even before he invited himself aboard the post-Chicago portion of her 1908 tour. She had been attracted to men before, but never had she been so "thrilled" by the touch of a man. Yet there was something about Reitman that she did not trust. His involvement in the subterfuge regarding her Workmen's Hall appearance nagged at her. Why had she acted so impulsively when caution should have been in order?

The year before meeting Reitman, Goldman confided to a fellow anarchist that she was "too much" a woman for her own good. "That's my tragedy," she wrote. Wanting to be both a woman and a revolutionary, she worried that she was "too much" a woman to be a revolutionary and "too relentless" a revolutionary to achieve any lasting personal happiness.

In the same year that Goldman defined her "tragedy," Reitman described himself as an "American by birth, a Jew by parentage, a Baptist by adoption, single by good fortune, a physician and teacher by profession, cosmopolitan by choice, a socialist by inclination, a rascal by nature, a celebrity by accident, a tramp of twenty years experience, and a Tramp Reformer by inspiration." Nowhere in that impish litany did he suggest that he had ever been an anarchist, whether by choice, nature, or inclination. That he was a "rascal" Goldman would discover shortly after their first meeting.

Preparations for the Workmen's Hall lecture proceeded smoothly enough. Word of Goldman's surreptitious appearance passed quietly among the city's radicals. On the appointed evening Goldman gained entrance to the hall without being detected by police. A large, friendly crowd had gathered, ostensibly to hear music. At a prearranged moment, Reitman announced that an old friend wanted to greet them. That was Goldman's cue to mount the podium. Before the ovation for her had subsided, police charged the stage intent on removing her from it. For a moment, confusion reigned. Goldman, her dress torn by an overeager law officer, had the presence of mind to call out to her followers: "The police are here to cause another Haymarket riot. Don't give them a chance. Walk out quietly and you will help our cause a thousand times more." The audience spontaneously left the hall "in perfect order."

On her way out, and in the firm grip of a police captain, Goldman turned in time to see Reitman being dragged into the night. When he passed her "without a look or a word," Goldman could only hope that he was trying to dupe his captors. Assuming no arrests, he surely would rejoin her and her entourage at their scheduled postlecture party.

When the police failed to file any charges, the gathering went ahead as planned—minus Reitman. As the night wore on, his absence grew more conspicuous by the hour. Goldman spent a "wretched evening" defending "the doctor" ("He must have been detained by the police . . . "), clinging to her dwindling faith in him, and yet fearing that he was, in fact, the source of the leak.

As it turned out, "the doctor" had not been arrested. Early the next morning he called on Goldman, but offered no good reason for his failure to appear the night before. Goldman "looked searchingly at him, trying to fathom his soul." Still no answer. Despite his silence, her doubts rapidly "melted like ice at the first rays of sun." No one "with such a frank face," she decided, could be capable of . . . deliberate lies."

A few days later the two were relaxing at a local restaurant when Goldman noticed that seated near them was a police captain who had arrested and bullied her following the McKinley assassination. To her amazement, the captain signaled for Reitman to join him. To her shock, "the doctor" did. "Anger, disgust, and horror" thrashed about in Goldman's head, while the captain's friendly "Hello, Ben" rang in her ears. All her doubts about whether or not Reitman was the Workmen's Hall informant resurfaced: "Was it possible?"

Needing time and separation to sort out her thoughts, Goldman decided to continue her tour alone. Pleading telegrams sought her out in hotel rooms from Minneapolis to Winnipeg and back. Finally, she decided to pay attention to her heart, rather than to her "rebellious brain." Even if Reitman was the informer, why shouldn't she be able to "carry him with me to the world of my social ideal"?

A one-word telegram to Chicago followed: "Come."

When Reitman arrived in Minneapolis he explained that he knew any number of policemen because of his work among the tramps and prostitutes of Chicago. Once again Goldman's doubts melted: "I had to believe in him with an all-encompassing faith." For the next seven years she tried desperately to keep that faith, despite recurring evidence that it was sadly misplaced. Her "great hunger" to find a lover and a collaborator had been satisfied, at least for the time being. Having "craved life and love," having "yearned to be in the arms of a man who came from a world so unlike mine," Goldman was caught "in the torrent of an elemental passion I had never dreamed any man could arouse in me." At least for the time being.

Whether to prove his loyalty or recapture a version of the tramp life, Reitman signed on as Goldman's aide, manager, and advance man. Privately, of course, he continued to play a fourth role in her life. Revolutionaries and propagandists by day, lovers (and battlers) by night, Reitman and Goldman were on the road as much as half of every year between 1908 and 1915. All that time Goldman did her best to cultivate her public image and to preserve her shrinking private sphere. Happiness to her was a lecture before a large, appreciative crowd, a follow-up social gathering at which she held court, and a night of romance with Reitman. At times she resented being "public property," but she was happiest when she was a celebrity radical with a life—and a secret—to call her own. Had she had her way, no one would ever have known that her disheveled-looking factotum was also her lover. For a time, no one did.

And, for a longer period of time, the combination of Goldman's platform skills and Reitman's promotional talent made for one successful tour after another. Crowd estimates vary widely, but some hard evidence exists for those cities in which Goldman spoke in lecture halls (she preferred them to outdoor gatherings). For example, in San Francisco for two weeks in 1909 she attracted approximately 2,000 listeners a night. Even in remote Winnipeg she drew as many as 1,500 people for a single talk. Although her lectures on birth control and against war insured the largest crowds, she continued to offer a wide variety of topics, including "The Intermediate Sex," "Woman's Inhumanity to Man," and "Patriotism."

This last lecture Goldman had occasion to deliver in San Francisco, where she defined patriotism as justification for the training of "wholesale murderers." In her audience was a young, uniformed soldier named William Buwalda, who was ostensibly there to practice his stenographic skills. For this indiscretion he was court-martialed, convicted, and given a five-year prison sentence. So ridiculous was the Army's behavior that President Roosevelt intervened. No lover of anarchists and no hater of the military, Roosevelt ordered Buwalda's immediate release from prison. The soldier was not converted to anarchism by the experience, but following his dishonorable discharge (and full pardon) he disavowed a badge given to him for his service in the Philippines following the Spanish-American War.

Goldman did have the power to change people's lives, a power derived from a voice that Reitman compared to that of the "Angel Gabriel." That voice was at the peak of its power precisely during these years. Friends and allies variously recalled that life took on an "intense quality" when she was on the platform, that she "held before us the ideal of freedom," that she "removed despair from those who would otherwise be hopeless."

It was Goldman's belief that everyone in her audience was an anarchist at heart. If her listeners had not yet realized as much, it was her task to help them find their way, whether via her vision of the good life or her blast at the world around her, or whether courtesy of her captivating delivery, her rhetorical questions, or her razzing of the inevitable hecklers in her audiences. Sometimes she spoke too quickly to be understood. Certainly, she spoke too rapidly for transcription. Always she had a standing offer to any detective or reporter present: If they could record her every word, she'd give them a kiss.

Neither local authorities nor the federal government were lulled into believing that Goldman was just another public entertainer. To them, she remained a dangerous anarchist for whom free love meant something more than a wagered kiss. Intent upon removing her from the United States, the Taft administration canceled her citizenship in 1909. Three years earlier Congress had passed a law withdrawing any citizenship obtained illegally. Suddenly, old rumors that Jacob Kersner had once lied about his age acquired new importance. Armed with this new law, government agents tracked down members of Kersner's family. If his age when he applied for citizenship in 1884 was wrongly given, perhaps so was his compliance with the five-year residency requirement. Documentation, however obtained, had new clout: Stripping him of citizenship would now deny her claim to the same. So, without ever contacting Kersner or the woman who twice divorced him, the government declared both Kersner and Goldman noncitizens. This official status did not mean that she would be subject to immediate removal from the United States, but she knew it might result in her being denied reentry if she ever chose so much as to travel abroad. Hence her self-declared status as a "prisoner in America."

Almost immediately, the government's action had its effect. A planned Goldman-Reitman tour of Australia had to be canceled. Originally scheduled for January 1909, the trip had already been postponed twice, owing to financial problems and the death of Goldman's father. By the spring the tour had to be put on hold again. Goldman took many risks in her life, but the risk of being permanently barred from the country of her choice was not one of them.

In some respects, Goldman's decision was a difficult one. Both she and Reitman had looked forward to a change in routine and terrain. Reitman was well aware that many of her allies did not trust him. (Berkman, for one, accused him of being a hypocrite without any "rebel spirit.") Goldman hoped that the trip would cure "the doctor" of his wandering eye. As early as the fall of 1908, Reitman confessed to her that he had not only stolen money from funds earmarked for *Mother Earth* but had had numerous fleeting affairs with other women. Goldman was devastated. Having believed that his "boyish irresponsible pranks" were over, she could not ignore this violation of trust that tore at her "very vitals."

The harder Goldman tried to deny Reitman's promiscuity, the more it gnawed at her. Just before he delivered his news, she had felt so thoroughly married that she called herself an "unhappy wife." The anarchist as monogamist? An unlikely combination perhaps, but it described her at that moment. Feeling so monogamous, so wifely, she had begun to question not only her commitment to anarchism, but her reputation as an independent woman. Then came the "doctor's" tearful confession.

Intellectually, Goldman believed in sexual variety; politically, she endorsed free love. But emotionally, she was so in love with Reitman that she longed for no one else. "I wish I could still be an arch-varietist," she confessed, but those days were "gone." When the subject turned to free love, she had to admit that her understanding of the concept did not match his. To her, free love implied love without legal marriage. To him, it meant lovemaking at will. At the same time, Goldman was consistent enough — and honest enough — to concede that she could not attack Reitman on political or moral grounds. She also had come to realize that she could not change him: "You will have your obsessions as long as you live."

Still, Goldman felt "worn out" by those obsessions — worn out and wounded by his "irresponsible, unscrupulous attitude toward women." She was also outraged and stunned by the consummation of one of his affairs in their "secret" apartment, and stunned and victimized by a lover who had destroyed her faith in the possibilities of love.

Reduced to pleading with Reitman to "give me back my faith," Goldman thought she had no alternative but to play on his sense of guilt. The problem was that Reitman had no sense of guilt when it came to his amatory life. Even though she did not consider herself "less sexed" than he, Goldman had been faithful to him out of her love for him. Reitman, in turn, was more confused than impressed by her loyalty.

In attempting to resolve his quandary, Goldman the victim became Goldman the teacher. Convention, she insisted, was not the issue. In fact, she admitted to the "doctor" that she could never tolerate a normal marital relationship. "Torment" was as natural to her life as dullness was to the lives of so many others. Claiming, therefore, that she did "not expect [him] to be conventional," she proceeded to give Reitman a lesson in her understanding of free love: "Your love is all sex, with nothing but indifference left when it is gratified. . . . My love is sex, but it is also devotion, care, anxiety, patience, friendship, it is all. . . . You are always primitive and I am hyper-civilized . . . [therein] lies the chasm."

Goldman's answer was love, not marriage, which "inhibits love." Only love could produce "true equality" between two people. Love, however, led neither to equality nor stability between Goldman and Reitman. Love only left her emotionally bruised by the "wounds" that he had inflicted. But then, "most people live with dead souls; why not I?" concluded Goldman, at her victimized best.

When it came to Reitman, this victim was always ready for more punishment. Life with him or without him was a "hideous nightmare." Again, Goldman entertained the idea of traveling to Australia, this time alone, until she realized that she would "probably never again know such a love" as Reitman. At least that is what a "sad and lonely Mommy" wrote to "baby mine" in the winter of 1909. Out of that loneliness, she invited him to come to New York. Out of his free love for her, he came.

For all of his obsessions, Reitman did love Goldman. He hated New York City and the people who called it home, especially the New York radical crowd. He saw himself as the permanent outsider among them, especially among the immigrant anarchists who still comprised Goldman's inner circle. What's more, he loved Chicago, where he had a home, a mission, and a following. He also had a mother there, a manipulative, guilt-inducing woman able to match Goldman threat for threat, tear for tear, sigh for sigh. Yet he left Chicago for New York, because his "sad and lonely Mommy" wanted him by her side.

Goldman was determined to bring consistency to her public and private lives. She wanted to be free to challenge the strictures of Victorian America, both from the platform and in her bedroom. As a result, she began to deal more directly in her lectures and writings with the war between the sexes. In a talk on the "White Slave Traffic," Goldman accused men of viewing women as objects of "mere sex gratification." A few years earlier she had attacked feminists for not opening themselves up to the possibilities of love. Having made herself vulnerable, she was now just as likely to accuse men of using women as prostitutes, lovers, or wives. In her mind, all three were virtually indistinguishable, and all were equally disposable victims of male lust.

Life with Reitman led Goldman to question publicly whether a woman could have a positive relationship with a man. At the same time, she was an avowed heterosexual. During one of her interludes without Reitman, she had occasion to meet one Almeda Sperry, a lesbian who made overtures to her to be her lover. Sperry, herself a reformed prostitute, had listened to the "White Slave Traffic" lecture and agreed with the revised Goldman view of men. "Nearly all men try to buy love," she wrote. "If they don't do it by marrying, they do it otherwise, and that is why I have such contempt for men. . . . I've seen too much and I am no fool."

Fool or no, Sperry did express her love for Goldman. It is doubtful that Goldman reciprocated in any physical sense. The two women shared their distrust of men, but they did not have similar sexual agendas or inclinations. Nonetheless, Goldman took great pride in giving lectures that "set people free" sexually. More than a few lesbians approached her with their "pitiful stories" of "social ostracism," making the life of the "invert more dreadful" than she had ever realized. Still, to her, anarchism offered a solution, because it was a a "living influence to free us from inhibitions." But Goldman, whom Sperry chided for being "strangely innocent," could not offer herself as a role model.

Sperry was also frustrated by the sheer number of people in Goldman's life and by the singularity of her commitment to anarchism. "At times," she conceded, "my hatred of you is greater than my love. I hate that your interests are myriad . . . that your cause is first." Her anger aside, Sperry's friendship with Goldman did reinforce their shared belief in free love. But Goldman could never overcome her suspicion that sexual intimacy between two women represented an unfortunate retreat from intimacy with men. Her anger at Reitman aside, she could never bring herself to ask him to leave her forever. To Sperry she wrote civilly; to Reitman she wrote passionately. He was always near the top of the "myriad" of interests that stood in Sperry's way.

Reitman, the "cruelest creature in the whole world," also stood in the way of Goldman's happiness. This woman, who had a keen sense of her own strength and superiority, was a "trembling leaf" in his presence. This believer in her innate ability to love more freely and overcome jealousy more readily than other mortals found herself playing out the "same coarse vulgar scenes of the ordinary herd." Still, she preferred the chaos of life with Reitman to the emptiness of life without him: "If I had to give up everything and everybody in order to go with Ben I would go. . . . He is the most compelling element in my life."

During the winter of 1910–1911, Goldman even thought she might be pregnant. For the first time in her life, she found herself dreaming of a home to share with the man in her life. There was no pregnancy, however, and there would be no home, "because I know you are happier in the cave."

Resigned to life as a single woman, Goldman once more sought happiness on the lecture circuit. Through the early spring of 1911, she traveled to fifty cities in eighteen states, giving at least 150 talks. She returned to New York more depressed than exhilarated. Reitman had gone home to Chicago—and to other women. "To you," she wrote, women are "like whiskey to the drunkard."

Nothing proceeded smoothly. Anarchism was at so low an ebb that Goldman considered "killing" *Mother Earth.* No one was living up to her standards—not the workers, not the middle class, not Reitman, not even an obsessed Goldman. "You are like anarchism to me. The more I struggle for it, the further it grows away from me." But struggle on she did, exploring the "secret joys and ecstasies of sex," wanting to be rid of her "hideous feeling of doubt," clutching to the notion that "dreams are the only things worth holding on to, and consoled by the thought that the "struggle" for liberty was more important that its attainment.

That struggle moved to new battlegrounds in 1912. The year began with plans for another tour, the theme of which soon narrowed to the unfolding events in Lawrence, Massachusetts. There 25,000 textile workers, most of them women and children, had gone on strike to block management's demand for a wage cut and a worker speedup. A new law had gone into effect limiting female and child workers to a fifty-four hour workweek. Previous such reductions had not led to corresponding wage cuts. But not this time. The result was a spontaneous walkout.

Over the years, unions had made little headway in the mills of Lawrence. In 1912 only 10 percent of the 30,000 to 35,000 workers belonged to trade unions. When the IWW came into being in 1905, it targeted Lawrence for organizing. Yet at the time of the strike only 300 workers were card-carrying Wobblies. Still, the IWW moved quickly to take command of the strike. Within two weeks Big Bill Haywood himself was in Lawrence to lead it. At forty-three, Haywood was a former mine worker who had grown more radical with age. Even his enemies had to concede that he was a leader able to appeal personally to workers of all types and radicals of all persuasions, including Emma Goldman.

She praised both the strike and what she hoped was a budding marriage between workers and radical intellectuals. Young rebels had flocked to Lawrence in support of strikers who had bannered the city with the slogan "We want bread and roses, too." For them, the staff of life meant more than just food on their plates; it also offered the opportunity to participate in a life of culture and beauty. This was the "lyrical left" in action. Their appeal was similar to a young Goldman's entreaties before Leopold Garson a quarter of a century earlier. Her demands then were their demands now.

Heartened by their stand, Goldman used her platform to raise money for a strike that married Haywood's "direct action" tactics to less traditional challenges to the mill owners. Young writers, artists, and intellectuals gathered in this aging textile town to organize everything from a "children's crusade" to soup kitchens to parades. Hundreds of Lawrence children were sent to live in temporary foster homes in New York City. Not only did their removal ease the relief problem, but the sight of refugee trains arriving at Grand Central Station attracted much-needed favorable national publicity. In addition, the strike committee channeled worker unrest into organized non-violence. Banners and parades replaced rocks and fists. Owing to such tactics—and to worker solidarity—the strike was a success. On March 12 the largest employer, the American Woolen Company, agreed to wage increases of 5 to 25 percent, with the largest increases targeted for the lowest paid workers.

Goldman praised the settlement without ever making the pilgrimage to Lawrence. Cheering the workers on from many points west, she rationalized that her contribution was on the platform. Moreover, she was pleased by the cooperation between intellectuals and workers at Lawrence. So far as she was concerned, intellectuals were members of the proletariat, whether they realized it or not. Intellectuals who had actually left their "pedestals" to go to Lawrence drew her longest accolades. But Goldman chose not to be among them. Perhaps she could not escape from her speaking commitments, or perhaps she preferred not to be too closely identified with particular strikes. Once again her status as an independent anarchist was at stake.

At the same time, some anarchists worried that their movement was becoming too middle class, too concerned with cultural issues, too isolated from labor. Voltairine de Cleyre, who died rather suddenly in 1912, had been critical of Goldman for cultivating "respectable audiences." Instead of focusing her energies on the "poor and the disinherited," de Cleyre accused Goldman of migrating from one "extravagant" hotel to the next, all the while building around herself a cult of personality.

Goldman pled guilty to spending time with "so-called respectable" people, because "pioneers" for anarchism were more likely to be found among them than in tenements or union halls. Moreover, her appeal was directed at individuals, not at classes. After all, she argued, the goal of anarchism was to surmount the class struggle, not to perpetuate it.

Curiously, Goldman ignored the charge that she put self-promotion ahead of advancing a movement. She refused to apologize for keeping her vision of anarchism both vague and futuristic. The lesson taught her years earlier by that anonymous Cleveland worker had never really taken hold. She would speak before IWW or Women's Trade Union League meetings, but never would she allow herself to be trapped by the routine or agenda of any organization.

Ironically, preaching that intellectuals were workers too, Goldman actually widened the gap between her vision of anarchism and the demands of workers for a better life now. In truth, she preferred the company of intellectuals. Among them, she was sure, were her "pioneers," while among the workers were all too many "ordinary men." Hence her decision to keep some distance between herself and the heat of battle in such places as Lawrence.

Although she admired the "direct action" tactics of the Wobblies more than the ballot box approach of the socialists, Goldman remained an anarchist. She may well have regretted staying away from Lawrence, but stay away she did. The goals of a strike were inevitably too limited. Therefore, she seldom felt compelled to link her arms or her cause with strikers.

In May 1912, Goldman did travel to San Diego with Reitman to support the right of dissenters to speak and organize in that city. Here local anarchists and Wobblies were united in a campaign to overturn an ordinance banning outdoor speeches and rallies. By the time the two outsiders arrived, the city was in the "grip of a veritable civil war." Some eighty-four men and women had already been arrested and jailed. Vigilantes had raided Wobbly headquarters, beating their quarry and forcing them to kiss the flag. On May 7, Wobbly Joseph Mikolsek was killed by police gunfire shortly after testing the speaking ban.

While in the city, Goldman did not get near a speaker's platform. In fact, she got little further than her hotel, which was surrounded by a mob of vigilantes. At that point the mayor paid a courtesy call. "They mean business," he told Goldman. "They want you out of the hotel. . . . We cannot guarantee anything. If you consent to leave, we will give you protection and get you safely out of town."

Goldman was not impressed by the offer. "Why don't you disperse the crowd?" she asked. The mayor refused.

"Very well, then, let me speak to them," Goldman shot back. "I could do it from a window here. I have faced infuriated men before, and I have always been able to pacify them." Again the mayor declined.

Now it was Goldman's turn to say no. Accepting police protection was never her practice, she interjected. With that, she stormed out of her room in search of Reitman. He was nowhere to be found.

Not until the middle of the night did Goldman learn Reitman's whereabouts. According to the house detective, Reitman was on a train headed for Los Angeles. Two hours later,
Goldman was on the next train north. When she arrived at
the Los Angeles depot, Reitman was not there. Convinced that
he had been killed, she went to the apartment where they
usually stayed when they were in the city. There she waited
and brooded until she received an anonymous phone call the
next afternoon informing her that Reitman was alive. He would
be arriving shortly by train from San Diego, and, "oh yes,"
the caller added, "his friends should bring a stretcher to the
station."

This last piece of advice was appropriate. When Goldman
finally saw Reitman, she was horrified. His body was a "mass
of bruises covered with blotches of tar. The letters IWW were
burned into his flesh." What had happened? Silence. Only
several hours later did he choose to talk. Escorted from the
hotel by seven men with drawn revolvers, he was taken on
a "frightful" ride out of the county. At that point, he was ordered from the car and stripped. His buttocks were branded
with the letters IWW. The men poured tar over his head and
rubbed sagebrush over his body. They forced him to kiss the
flag, sing the national anthem, and run a gauntlet of kicking
feet and flailing fists. Only then did they release Reitman, clad
this time in his underwear and a vest, which contained his
money, his watch, and a railroad ticket.

The San Diego episode forever affected the relationship
between Goldman and Reitman. Although their touring and
lovemaking continued, he was no longer the same confident,
boastful person. Convinced that "most of him died" on that
single torturous night, he grew preoccupied with his failure
to fight back. If only he had stood up to them. If only he hadn't
been afraid. If only Goldman could accept him for what he had
revealed himself to be.

But Goldman could not. What galled her was not so much
Reitman's momentary cowardice, but his open acknowledg-
ment of it. So shameless was he that he exposed his IWW
brand at one of their lecture stops. It was one thing to have
acted the coward; it was quite another to "herald your action

as cowardly." If Reitman felt that way, Goldman preferred that he keep it to himself. No "woman who loves a man, especially the woman who has all her life faced persecution, [wants] to hear that man shout from the house tops, he is a coward."

Goldman could be many things to Reitman, but she could never be indifferent. Prior to San Diego, she had never held him in contempt. After San Diego, that feeling crept into her consciousness. In addition, the sexual tables had suddenly turned. Now Goldman began to hint of new amorous interests, and now Reitman worried that his sexual potency had diminished. To be a coward was bad enough; to be an impotent coward was far worse—in his eyes and in hers.

Now it was Reitman's turn to prove himself to Goldman. In the summer, he left his mother for Goldman and New York. She wanted a faithful lover. He promised to be just that. Soon, however, the same frictions kindled into rage; the old hurts produced new bruises. Reitman may have been temporarily chastened by his encounter with tar and sagebrush, but his bravado in the bedroom soon returned.

Goldman spent the fall trying once again to forget about Reitman and his hollow promises. And Alexander Berkman helped her forget. His *Prison Memoirs* needed editing, and she volunteered her services. The contrast between these two men was too stark for Goldman to ignore. Reading Berkman's story reminded her of his bravery, his deed, and his years of punishment and stoic resolve behind bars. Suddenly, Berkman was once again the model revolutionary. He had held to his ideals, even at the risk of physical pain. Reitman had had pain inflicted upon him, but for what purpose? He had always put his pleasure before her revolution.

Reitman was not ready to put Goldman behind him. Over the winter of 1912–1913, he grew obsessed with the idea of returning to San Diego. Despite her considerable reservations, Goldman agreed to accompany him. This time, he promised, things would be different. And they were. This time the two were arrested immediately. With vigilantes surrounding the jail chanting "We want Reitman," he was reduced to quavering incoherence. His fear was so palpable that Goldman decided they ought to leave as quickly as possible, even if it meant accepting an embarrassing police escort. From that day forward, it "grieved" Goldman to realize that Reitman was "not made of heroic stuff."

Within the year, however, the two were again living together. This time, in New York's Harlem, Goldman deliberately set out to create a communal household. The old Greenwich Village apartment had become little more than a "home of lost dogs." This time Goldman would select her housemates carefully. The list included Reitman and his mother (his room would be closer to his "Mommy's" than to his mother's), Berkman, Eleanor Fitzgerald (who was both a friend of Goldman's and a former lover of Reitman's and Berkman's), a niece and a nephew of Goldman's, a few select members of the *Mother Earth* staff, and Goldman herself. The arrangement was a recipe for psychological disaster. Within a few months, the tension had reached the explosion point. More Reitman promiscuity and more Reitman confessions were followed by flying chairs and words, both hurled by Goldman. Without a word, or a chair, in response, Reitman and his mother left for Chicago. Never again did the three (or two) attempt to live together under the same roof.

Reitman left with "no plans, no hope, no ambition, no sweetheart needing me." But Goldman did need him – on the road. Their "only happiness" had been achieved on tour, so Reitman told her that "if you really love me and want to work with me again, you can go ahead with arrangements." When pressed to explain why she decided to reunite the team, Goldman could only offer a Russian aphorism: "If you drink, you'll die, and if you don't drink, you'll die. Better to drink and die." Better to lecture and live.

By 1914, Goldman was on the road once more. With war about to erupt in Europe, she spoke out against militarism in all its nationalistic guises. With war already a reality in the mining camps of the American West, she railed against the violence of the mine owners. With war between the sexes a never-ending battle, she decided to promote birth control in the name of "free motherhood."

Her private life a shambles, Goldman returned to the public wars with a renewed sense of purpose. "Tired of feeding leeches," she wanted only to "have a nook for myself" as she prepared for a new round of speaking engagements. Meanwhile, the all-too-predictable Reitman became inexplicably unpredictable. Worried that Goldman was spending too much time with Sperry, he questioned her sexuality. That drew this exasperated, yet plaintive, response: "I do not incline that way. I love your damned sex . . . I don't know why I love you, but I know how I love you."

Did she love him enough to become his wife and the mother of his children? Reitman asked. Goldman was dumbfounded. She was as unable to believe him as she was unwilling to marry him. Instead she was ready to launch a new campaign.

Goldman had learned of advanced methods of birth control during her travels in Europe in the late 1890s. But she had refused to discuss specific practices publicly, because she did not want to risk arrest for this issue alone. The 1873 Comstock Law had made it illegal to mail "obscene, lewd, or lascivious articles." Courts had subsequently included birth control devices, as well as public discussion of their uses, within this mandate. Hence her reluctance to speak on the subject. The fear of prison did not give her pause. She had been there before, and she was willing to go there again. But she did not consider advocacy of birth control worth a return trip to Blackwell's Island.

Instead, Goldman challenged mainline feminists by holding women responsible for many of the ills that beset them. Mothers, for example, had only themselves to blame for raising sons to become tyrants: "The mother leaves nothing undone to keep her son tied to her. Yet she hates to see him weak, and she craves a manly man. She idolizes in him the very traits that help to enslave her—his strength, his egotism, and his exaggerated vanity." It was the "inconsistencies of my sex" that kept the "poor male dangling between . . . the darling and the brute."

Nor did Goldman see women as morally superior to men. Many suffragists had asserted this brand of superiority to buttress their demand for the vote. Goldman, however, denied both the importance of the vote and this argument to obtain it. Privately, she could accuse Reitman of preferring the "cave." Privately, he was the "primitive" and she was "hyper-civilized." But publicly she saw no differences, moral or otherwise, between the sexes. Women, she argued, should not be given the vote because they were better, more socially conscious human beings. Women should vote only to have "as much chance to make a fool of [themselves] as men have had."

All of this was standard Goldman fare on women, until 1914 and the publication of Margaret Sanger's magazine *The Woman Rebel*. To Sanger, the issue of birth control (which was a term that she had coined) was a matter of life and death for great numbers of poor women. To Goldman, the issue was primarily a free speech concern. Discussion of birth control was a taboo to be eliminated, not a cause to be championed, and certainly not *the* cause beyond all others.

Sanger's priorities were no doubt attributable to her background. She was born into a large, working-class, Catholic family. When she was sixteen, her mother died of tuberculosis, complicated by cervical cancer, following the birth of eleven children. Like Goldman, she later studied to be a nurse and ministered to the poor immigrant families of New York. Unlike Goldman, she not only worked closely with both socialists and Wobblies, but toiled in the union trenches, including a stint helping to organize the exodus of strikers' children from Lawrence in 1912. Also unlike Goldman, she was willing to challenge directly the detested Comstock Law. In August 1914, Sanger was arrested for publishing birth control instructions in a pamphlet called "Family Limitation," 100,000 copies of which had been distributed by the IWW. Rather than stand trial, Sanger fled to Europe. Nonetheless, Goldman remained supportive of Sanger's work in the pages of *Mother Earth*. Perhaps spurred by Sanger's arrest, or perhaps fearful of being upstaged, Goldman decided to include birth control information in her upcoming round of lectures. Within the year she, too, was arrested. Charged with violating the New York State Penal Code, which made it a misdemeanor to advertise or distribute "any recipe, drug, or medicine for the prevention of conception," she faced the very jail sentence she had long sought to avoid.

In the meantime, relations between the two women soured considerably. By now, each regarded the other as her chief rival for leadership of the birth control movement. Goldman accused Sanger of ingratitude for her past support. Sanger, in turn, wrongly charged *Mother Earth* with silence on the subject of her arrest.

Never one to flee a fight, Goldman decided to use her trial to promote her case for birth control. Waiving counsel, she contended that large families were a "millstone" around the necks of American workers. Neither men nor women dared to strike with many mouths to feed. Furthermore, men now wanted women to be more than breeders of children. If previous generations of feminists had sought to free women from sex, Goldman saw nothing wrong in freeing women *for* sex.

Shifting to a different line of argument, Goldman insisted that poor women ought to have access to information that women with money had no trouble acquiring. All women, rich and poor, ought to have only as many children as they desired. Birth control offered that prospect. Was she a criminal for saying as much? Not when children were being destroyed by capitalism and war. Not when she was simply working for "healthy motherhood and happy child-life." Not for telling women that they "need not always keep their mouths shut and their wombs open." If such language made her a criminal, she told the judge, then she was "proud to be considered a criminal."

Minus Goldman's pride, the judge agreed. He sentenced her to either fifteen days in jail or a $100 fine. She chose the time. On April 20, "Our Lady of Sorrows" (Reitman's appellation) entered Queens County Jail. From her cell she wrote a female ally that it would be "well if every rebel were sent to prison for a time." The experience would fan one's "smoldering flame of hate of the things that make prisons possible." Perhaps she was recalling her months on Blackwell's Island twenty-two years earlier, as well as Sanger's flight to Europe to avoid prosecution and jail.

Upon her release, Goldman was greeted at Carnegie Hall with a celebration in her honor, a celebration that marked the recognition that birth control was no longer a "mere theoretical issue." From that point on, it became for Goldman an "important phase of the social struggle." The sole "disturbing element" of the affair was the refusal of socialist Max Eastman to preside if Reitman was allowed to speak, all of which was proof to Goldman that some "alleged radicals" had a poor understanding of the "true meaning of freedom."

Goldman relished her freedom so much that she was not anxious to return to jail. No longer would she distribute circulars on birth control methods. Instead, she would confine herself to "oral information" in her lectures on "Free or Forced Motherhood." Jail was not so valuable an experience that she was anxious for a return engagement over an issue that she still did not regard as *that* critical. Content to leave the field to those who saw birth control as the "only panacea for all social ills," she was ready to move on to more "vital" issues.

Goldman refused to make her peace with Sanger. On economic and labor issues, she had been accused by de Cleyre and others of ignoring the workers and selling out to the "respectable" middle class. On the birth control front, she leveled similar charges at Sanger. In her fervor to gain support for birth control, Sanger had grown more conservative, by either failing to take a stand on other issues or by pitching her appeal to middle-class parents who wanted to limit their families. When Goldman did look beyond the free speech dimension of birth control, she focused on the problems faced by poor, largely immigrant families. In sum, the birth control issue proved to be Goldman's vehicle for restoring her reputation as a left-wing anarchist.

It also provided a way for Goldman to reconnect her life with Reitman's. During 1915 and 1916 he played a key role in the widening campaign for birth control. As a physician, he had long been concerned about the medical aspects of the problem, particularly the link between venereal disease and birth defects. He, too, distributed illegal pamphlets. He, too, was arrested. And he, too, was slighted by Sanger, which to Goldman was an "inexcusable breach of solidarity." At roughly the same time that Goldman was sent to jail, Reitman was put on trial. In short order, he was convicted and sentenced to sixty days in the workhouse. Two subsequent convictions in 1917 and 1918 resulted in a $1,000 fine and a six-month jail term.

Despite the communality of their interest, the two were not fully reconciled. For a time they were brought closer together, but Reitman was desirous of finding a mate and settling down, and Goldman was unwilling to be that mate—for Reitman or for anyone else.

Reitman had been "seduced" by the "ordinary man's" dream of a home and a family. Goldman remained caught up in her "struggle to maintain [her] own individuality." This was not the time to retire from the platform—not while the private wars between the sexes raged in post-Victorian America; not while labor wars dotted the American landscape; not while a world war consumed Europe and threatened to engulf America; and not while she could still command an audience. For better or for worse, Goldman had made her choice. Trapped in the role of celebrity radical, she evidenced no interest in plotting her escape.

CHAPTER EIGHT

At War Against War

It was almost as though everything in Goldman's American life pointed toward 1917 and the fateful American decision to send an army to Europe. In April, President Woodrow Wilson asked Congress to declare war against Germany and "make the world safe for democracy." Waging war abroad was only half the battle. Within weeks of the vote for war, the Wilson administration declared war on its domestic opponents of war, Goldman prominently among them. For the nearly three years of its European life, Goldman had publicly opposed both the war and U.S. participation in it. Long before Wilson asked for war, she assumed he wanted war. Therefore, when not spreading the virtues of birth control and free love, she was traveling the country to rail against all "Promoters of the War Mania," Wilson prominently among them.

Many radicals had supported Wilson's 1916 reelection bid, but Goldman was not among them. They took seriously the Democratic campaign slogan, "He Kept Us Out of War." She did not. Still, many radicals and reformers marched behind Wilson and peace in 1916. Goldman, of course, supported peace, but she could never endorse Wilson, let alone vote for him.

Wilson had repeatedly told the American people that both "freedom of the seas" and "American honor" in its defense were at stake. In *Mother Earth*, Goldman countered with a question—How much freedom of the seas did the masses ever enjoy? — and an answer — Only the "exploiters" benefited from this bogus "freedom." She also responded with a speculation: The war would have ended "long ago" had the "American financiers been prevented from investing billions in war loans."

Proud of her challenge to Wilson, Goldman regarded her antiwar activities as her "best and most important work." At least that was her judgment from the vantage point of July, 1917, and her conviction for "conspiring" against the military draft. Never once did she believe that this was a war for democracy. If anything, it was a war that made a mockery of democracy; if anything else, it was a war to make the world safe for capitalism. She had "'never been more sure" of anything in her long public life. Therefore, Goldman felt compelled to declare her own war against war. Failing that, she waged her own version of a guerrilla war against the U.S. war effort. The U.S. government was swift to launch a counterattack of its own against the most visible and vocal symbol of the opposition to what would soon become "Mr. Wilson's War."

The guns of August 1914 had barely commenced firing when Goldman began to speak out against one more "capitalist war." A self-described "antimilitarist," rather than a pacifist, her opposition to this or any war between nations was not based on a philosophy of nonviolence. "The ordinary pacifist merely moralizes; the antimilitarist acts; he refuses to be ordered to kill his brothers." Revolutionary violence carried out by brothers and sisters against "capitalist governments" was generally understandable and often defensible; official violence by "capitalist governments" was not. Whether a national army was deployed against domestic strikers or foreign soldiers made no difference to her. Both actions were wrong. But after August 1914, not all of her anarchist comrades agreed. For example, Kropotkin, much to Goldman's dismay, supported the Allies, so fearful was he of a "Prussianized" Europe.

Less surprising, but no more pleasing to Goldman, was the failure of workers to spurn their national colors. Sustained by her belief that the masses had been wrong before, she took it upon herself to outline their "interests" and redefine "glory" for them. Taught by the state to fight for "national honor," they had to understand that "glory" meant "bleeding to death for the crooked transactions of a gang of legalized, cowardly thieves."

So, for the nearly three years that the United States was a nonbelligerent, Goldman had to direct her own belligerence at both the "war maniacs" in the Wilson administration and at the "dumb, suffering herd" willing to follow it. American workers had to be taught that they had a war of their own to fight in the mills and the mines, in the streets and country roads of the United States. A war of violence? Once again she drew back. Too much of the retaliatory violence was stupid violence. Angered by the "butchery" in a Rockefeller-owned mining camp in Ludlow, Colorado, which saw twenty-two people die at the hands of an unprovoked militia, she stood "aghast at the irresponsibility" of Rockefeller's enemies. In New York City three obscure anarchists managed to blow themselves up while preparing a bomb meant for those they deemed responsible for the Ludlow killings. When Goldman learned of the accident, she mixed sadness at their deaths with a blast against actions that inevitably "jeopardized innocent lives."

A few months later a full issue of *Mother Earth* explored the role of political violence. One article went so far as to endorse "offensive violence," especially dynamite, against the state. Echoing Johann Most, the author of this article, (who was unknown to Goldman) saw dynamite as the great equalizer in the war the oppressors. Goldman, upset with Berkman for running the essay, disavowed the entire issue, filled as it was with "prattle about force and dynamite." Everything in it should have been "thrown into the fire." Only violence targeted at specific oppressors (such as Frick and McKinley) was apparently defensible.

Two years later another bomb drew Goldman's attention. On July 22, 1916, San Francisco played host to a Preparedness Day parade. There, Goldman joined Berkman, who had recently migrated to the city to found a magazine, *The Blast*, directed exclusively at a working-class audience. Together they planned to speak against militarism. Her lecture had originally been scheduled for July 20, but she postponed it when she learned that it conflicted with meetings of labor groups. The new date was to have been the evening of July 22, but that night her San Francisco comrades heard no lecture. Earlier a bomb had exploded in mid-parade, killing eight people and wounding forty more. The next day four local labor leaders were arrested, and Berkman's office was raided.

In the days and weeks following the explosion, few radicals spoke up in defense of the four. The lesson of the McNamara brothers loomed too large for most of them. Six years earlier a bomb had ripped into the Los Angeles *Times* building. The defendants, J. J. and J. B. McNamara, were also labor organizers who protested their innocence. Radicals and reformers, socialists and anarchists, rallied to their support. Despite the efforts of Clarence Darrow, both brothers were convicted, after which they stunned their supporters by admitting their guilt. Angry, contorted faces suddenly gave way to silent, sheepish faces. The next time a dragnet caught suspected bombers there would be far fewer cries of support for the accused. Following the Preparedness Day explosion, Berkman and Goldman were almost alone in their defense of the indicted four.

Two of the four in particular, Thomas Mooney and Warren Billings, had had a long history of West Coast labor radicalism. Having come to know both of them, Berkman was convinced that they were being framed because of their labor work. Goldman barely knew either man, but she was willing to follow Berkman's lead. The bomb may not have been defensible, but the defendants were. Therefore, she cut short a Provincetown, Massachusetts, vacation to find a lawyer for Mooney and Billings. Her target was Frank P. Walsh, a reform-minded attorney who was deeply involved in President Wilson's reelection campaign. She finally located Walsh in Kansas City, only to have him reject her overtures in the name of Wilson's candidacy and peace. The first responsibility of those on the left, he instructed Goldman, was to keep the United States out of the war by retaining Woodrow Wilson in the White House. Again Goldman was unsurprised. Walsh's priorities were only "additional proof" of the "muddle-headedness of American liberals."

In the meantime, a New York Tammany Hall lawyer was secured for what proved to be an exercise in futility. In September 1916, Billings was sentenced to life in prison; the following February, Mooney was given the death penalty. On the heels of the Mooney verdict the San Francisco district attorney decided to go after Goldman and Berkman as well, claiming that the bomb plot had been concocted in Berkman's office.

Through the late winter and early spring of 1917, these two anarchists were fighting wars on two fronts. Now more of a team—and perhaps more intensely revolutionary—than they had been since Homestead, Goldman and Berkman found themselves simultaneously on the defensive and on the offensive. Worried about their own potential indictments for the July explosion, they moved to redouble their efforts to block U.S. entrance into the war.

Following the German decision to resume unrestricted submarine warfare in late January, the Wilson administration moved reluctantly, but inexorably, toward war. On the eve of actually delivering his war message to Congress, Wilson worried about the consequences of a vote for war. Still a cautious politician and not yet an isolated prophet, he sensed the depth of opposition to a U.S. military presence in Europe. He also was aware that his general willingness to tolerate dissent was severely limited. Now that the stakes had been raised significantly, he could be assured of dissent aplenty. Those dissenters would soon feel the consequences of the president's anger.

That anger was fed by Wilson's notion of majoritarian democracy. Once the people had spoken, in this case by way of a congressional declaration of war, there was no longer any room or reason for dissent. Therefore, official censorship was as legitimate as the commandeering of resources, including young men, for the ensuing fight.

Goldman was not deterred by either the president's anger or his argument. A crusader nearly all her life, she was suspicious of any government-sponsored crusades. The fact that this one threatened to take lives and torment dissenters only confirmed her old suspicions. Censorship and compulsion "always made me surer of myself."

In April 1917 the only question in Goldman's mind was whether to conduct her crusade in the United States or in Russia. The collapse of the monarchy a few weeks earlier raised her hopes for Russia. In a slightly different sense, it was 1892 or 1905 all over again: Should she stay in the United States or return to Russia? The question answered itself when she began to learn the fate of others who had already left for Russia. Reports began filtering in that American radicals bound for Russia were being detained in England and returned home. Apparently, the Allies were not anxious to release antiwar Americans into a country whose commitment to the war was tenuous and whose presence in the war remained vital.

One wonders whether Goldman's decision to stay had been all that difficult to make. The year 1917 was already shaping up to be the most significant year in her American life. Had she been *that* excited by the prospect of returning to Russia, she would have been part of the first migratory wave. Aside from the questionable status of her citizenship, she had two major reasons for staying behind: her attachment to the United States and her knowledge that there was plenty for her to do there. War fever was rampant, and there was an urgent need to inoculate Americans against it.

By mid-May all of Goldman's energy was directed at the Selective Service Act. Not since the Civil War had there been a military draft. Then the scandal was the lengthy list of approved exemptions and the legal hiring of substitutes. The Wilson administration sought to correct both inequities through a lottery. To Goldman the scandal of this draft was that it existed at all.

As political pressure for the draft built, Goldman and Berkman organized a No-Conscription League. On its letterhead, the League declared:

> We oppose conscription because we are internationalists, antimilitarists, and opposed to all wars waged by capitalistic governments.

Therefore, League members pledged to "resist conscription by every means in our power and sustain those who . . . refuse to be conscripted."

However, not all peace groups saw themselves as confirmed enemies of a wartime Wilson administration. For example, the Women's Peace Party, long an opponent of the war and America's participation in it, advocated halting all antiwar work. To Goldman, this stance was evidence of the worthlessness of organized feminism. With war at hand, this was the very time to challenge the state, not bow down before it.

Socialists and Wobblies, Goldman soon discovered, were little better. Officially, the Socialist Party of America was opposed to intervention, but prowar socialists were conspicuous in their support for Wilson. Once again, Goldman nodded knowingly. After all, these were people who had "trained the workers in obedience and patriotism, trained them to rely on parliamentary authority." In Germany, socialist leaders had "joined hands with the Kaiser." Why should their American counterparts be any different? All were "pseudo-radicals," who worshiped state power rather than personal freedom. None understood that only evil could come from orchestrated patriotism, commandeered soldiers, and silenced dissenters.

With the IWW, Goldman's fight was not against the leadership, which refused to abide by a wartime "no-strike" pledge, but with the vast majority of its membership, who trooped off to register for the draft. All this herdlike behavior on the part of brother and sister radicals only reaffirmed Goldman's own spirited sense of independence. In one way or another, to one degree or another, feminists, socialists, and unionists had all caved in to the demands of the state.

Not far behind were the intellectuals. Seduced either by the power of the state or by their own desire to wield power, many of them saw the war as an opportunity not to be missed. Dazzled by Roosevelt and his New Nationalism, they looked forward to the day when the state could hold its own against big business and big labor. Charmed by Wilson and his New Freedom, they followed their leader from his Jeffersonian origins to his Hamiltonian conclusions. Wilson may have been reluctant to preside over a permanently powerful central government, but by 1917 he seemed to have arrived at Roosevelt's destination and taken his fellow intellectuals with him.

Writing in *Mother Earth,* a young intellectual named Randolph Bourne concluded that this was a war "made deliberately by the intellectuals." Bourne had watched intellectuals, including ex-pacifists, ex-socialists, and ex-radicals, rid themselves of their pre–April 1917 convictions with amazing speed. They fell in line behind Wilson because they had a compelling "itch to be in the great experience." Anxious to be one with their nation, they wanted to feel important. In the process, they achieved a unique peacefulness, a state characterized by a British pacifist as the "peacefulness of being at war." By their behavior they revealed to Bourne that the real enemy was not Germany, but war itself.

On this point, Goldman agreed. So did Crystal Eastman and Roger Baldwin of the newly created Civil Liberties Bureau. An offshoot of the American Union Against Militarism (AUAM), the bureau continued to fight the draft even after the leadership of the AUAM had surrendered to Wilson. From 1914 on, the AUAM had taken a leading role in opposing U.S. entry into the war. In 1916 it supported Wilson and, it assumed, peace. Led by social reformers Lillian Wald and Paul Kellogg, the AUAM was a solidly respectable organization with many friends in high places. When war was declared over their objections, the leadership of the AUAM faced a critical choice: oppose the inevitable conscription of men and ideas or preserve their influence within official Washington. Wald and Kellogg selected the latter course, thereby forcing Eastman and Baldwin to break with the AUAM to found the Civil Liberties Bureau and fight the draft.

In possession of a puritan conscience and a Unitarian upbringing, Baldwin had been heading for a life of aimless gentility when a reform-minded lawyer and fellow Bostonian named Louis Brandeis encouraged him to spurn a business career for public service. At the still impressionable age of twenty-two, Baldwin followed that advice by becoming a social worker in the wilds of St. Louis. The year was 1906. Two years later he spent a Sunday afternoon listening to his first Emma Goldman lecture. Her "vision of the end of poverty and injustice," he later recalled, marked a "turning point" in his intellectual and political life.

Baldwin also credited Goldman with convincing him of the importance of freedom of speech. If so, he was once hesitant to support her exercise of that very freedom. In 1909 she wrote Baldwin to request use of his meeting hall. He declined apologetically: "We are slaves to public opinion and the goodwill of our subscribers." A year later Goldman was denied permission to speak at Washington University in St. Louis. This time Baldwin intervened privately on her behalf. He assured university officials that he had attended a number of her lectures, that her audiences were "distinctly high class," and that nothing "approximating a disturbance" had ever taken place. Boldness was not yet a Baldwin trait in 1909.

Seven years later, Baldwin's willingness to break with the AUAM was evidence that the Goldman influence had had some residual impact. With potential draftees streaming into the AUAM office, Baldwin and Eastman set up a Bureau of Conscientious Objectors. But they advised draft-age men not to evade registration: "Obedience to law, to the utmost limits of conscience, is the basis of good citizenship." At the same time, Baldwin informed War Secretary Newton Baker that he was "entirely at [his] service" in any joint effort to strike a compromise on the drafting of those opposed to military service.

Goldman's style was slightly more confrontational. During the course of its aborted six weeks of life, her No-Conscription League specialized in antidraft manifestos, mass meetings, and defiant rhetoric. It was, however, not in the business of offering advice to draft-age youth. The League's stated purpose was simply to stand by those who had already decided to refuse military service. One of its founders was not about to counsel anyone against compliance with the draft. After all, as an anarchist, Goldman could not pretend to tell others what to do; as a woman, she refused to tell men not to fight.

If Goldman hoped that this exercise in restraint would keep the government from shutting down the League, she was wrong. Its rallies and manifestos provided sufficient justification for the Wilson administration to act. On June 5 its most telling antidraft statement was published to coincide with national draft registration day, a day when American democracy was being "carried to its grave." Derisively titled "Holiday,"

it introduced a special issue of *Mother Earth*, some 20,000 copies of which were distributed despite Post Office Department
efforts to suppress it. Why did the government object so
strenuously? Goldman's opening lines provide a hint: "On June
5 the Moloch militarism will sit in pompous state awaiting its
victims who are to be dedicated to its gluttonous appe-
tite . . . the monster will reach out for the youth of the land
to be sacrificed on the altar of blood and iron." The "holiday"
was about to begin.

Still, nowhere in the issue did Goldman come close to
overtly instructing her readers to resist the draft. On the platform she followed a similar approach. More anti-Wilson than
was the AUAM, but less deferential than was Baldwin, she
shied away from taking the final step that would lead directly
to her arrest. Her task was to "make the issue plain"; her
listeners were entirely free to "act on their own."

This was a fine line to be drawing when the government
was drawing lines of its own. After three public rallies, the order for Goldman's arrest went out. On May 18, 8,000 people
(including soldiers and detectives) gathered at the Harlem River
Casino to hear Goldman and Berkman together on the same
platform for the first time in years. They also listened to a soldier defend the draft from the podium, thanks to Goldman
who refused to deny him his right to free speech. At Hunt's
Point Palace on June 4 the two anarchists spoke on the eve of
registration day. Amid cheers, boos, and flying lemons, Berkman defined conscription as the "cemetery of liberty." To him,
June 5 marked "black Tuesday," a day of "mourning" over lost
liberty.

Goldman was the last to speak. "Friends, workers, soldiers, detectives, and police," she began. Recalling the annual
military registration day in Russia, she reminded her listeners
that America was supposed to be a land where no one could
be compelled to be a soldier. Instead America was about to
conduct a "funeral march for 500,000 young men." Speaking
directly to the authorities in her audience, she urged them to
"have the decency" to admit that their actions in support of
the draft "will Prussianize America" in the name of democratiz-

ing Germany. Not a few hecklers shouted at Goldman and Berkman to go back to Russia. But Goldman would have none of it. Anarchism meant free choice. She had chosen America. No heckler would drive her form the platform or out of the country.

While Goldman was speaking, soldiers were throwing handfuls of freshly broken light bulbs on the platform. Some then threatened to storm it. At this point Goldman stopped and turned to the soldiers to thank them, sarcastically for providing "protection" to the assembled. If anyone prevented a full-scale riot that evening it was Goldman herself. Shouting amid the debris and the din, she warned her troops that the soldiers were there for one purpose only: to provoke a violent response from the assembled. Don't play into their hands, she urged. No one did.

On June 12, Federal Marshal Thomas McCarthy told the *New York Times* that he was ready to "arrest this Goldman woman if she organizes more meetings." Never one to back down from a threat, Goldman went ahead with a planned third meeting scheduled for June 14 at Forward Hall. It would be her last appearance for the No-Conscription League. Ironically, the decision to stop speaking was jointly hers and the government's. Having learned that agents were infiltrating her rallies to entrap nonregistrants, she vowed to limit her future League activities to the written word. The government had another idea. On June 15 she was arrested by McCarthy, who arrived at her office with seven deputies and a copy of the June 5 *Mother Earth*. Minutes later, Berkman was also taken into custody.

Without benefit of a search warrant, the marshal and his deputies proceeded to confiscate manuscripts, correspondence, subscription lists, books, and lecture notes, all the while searching for a document they prized above all others, the membership list of the No-Conscription League. No list was found. When Goldman asked to see their warrant, none was produced. Instead, McCarthy informed her that a warrant was superfluous. *Mother Earth* alone, he countered, contained enough "troublesome matter" to land her in jail for years. With that, recalled Goldman, her intruders hauled away a "wagon load" of documents (none of which she ever saw again).

The next morning Goldman and Berkman were formally charged with conspiring to "induce persons not to register" for the draft. The two were then held incommunicado, pending a benefactor coming forth to meet their $25,000 bail.

The right to a speedy trial is a constitutional guarantee, but little did this pair of defendants realize how quickly the prosecution intended to move. Goldman barely had time to read James Joyce's *Portrait of an Artist as a Young Man,* which she had stuffed into her handbag on the day of her arrest. On June 22 they were told that the trial would begin on June 27, which happened to be Goldman's forty-eighth birthday.

On the eve of the trial, Goldman was convinced that she was already"as good as convicted." She proved an accurate prophet. Despite her and Berkman's vigorous questioning, an unfriendly panel was selected for a jury. Berkman quizzed prospective jurors at length about their individual commitments to free speech. He also wanted to know whether those who would judge him operated on the general assumption that the majority was always right. Goldman concentrated on their reaction to her views on birth control, free love, and marriage. In the end the jury included no immigrants and no members of even a loosely defined working class.

The case against the two went beyond charges of "conspiracy" to include advocacy of violence, misappropriation of funds, and acceptance of German money. A detective-stenographer at Goldman's Harlem River Casino speech testified that she had said "we believe in violence and we will use violence." Goldman denied making the statement, but the precise truth will never be known. She usually hired her own stenographer, but none was present on this occasion. In cross-examination, she established that the prosecution's stenographer could take only one hundred words a minute, while demonstrating to the jury that she spoke in bursts much faster than that. At her insistence, a courtroom exercise revealed the stenographer's inability to keep pace with her. Stenography aside, the prosecution could still point to the infamous July

1914 issue of *Mother Earth* as proof of her commitment to violence.

The charge against Goldman and Berkman of enriching themselves at the expense of others was ludicrous. Their combined bank account at the time of the trial was $746.96. But the prosecution pressed them on a mysterious $3,000 gift. Such a bequest had been made, Goldman conceded. Its source turned out to be an eighty-year-old Swedish immigrant named James Hallbeck, who had made a good deal of money growing grapes in California. An anarchist since Haymarket, Hallbeck had simply walked unannounced into Goldman's *Mother Earth* office, check in hand. Goldman accepted the gift, which she immediately transferred to the No-Conscription League, not to her pocketbook.

Surprisingly little time was spent on the main charge of "conspiracy." Again, stenographic evidence had Goldman offering to "support the men who will refuse to register and who will refuse to fight." Again she claimed that her offer had extended only to those who had already rejected conscription on their own. She called a conscientious objector who testified that he had gone to the League office only to have her tell him that any draft-related decision was a matter of personal conscience. Office workers for the League testified that they had never heard anyone counsel a young man not to register.

In his final summation to the jury, Berkman conceded his opposition to registration and conscription, while denying that he and Goldman had "conspired" at all. "We are not the sort who shirk about, who hide here and there . . . Gentlemen, as to a conspiracy, there ain't no such animal in this zoo!" Berkman insisted that he possessed "no double character," that he always said the same thing publicly and privately. Did he tell anyone not to register? Never. Why not? "Because I would never advise anyone to do a thing which does not endanger me." (At forty-eight, he was well beyond the top draftable age of thirty.)

Berkman also challenged the veracity of the stenographer. "Emma is the third-fastest speaker in America. Only experts can take her speeches." This stenographer "left out the words he didn't get and put in the things he thought should be there." He wasn't a "bad man . . . just weak and a patrolman." If his alleged coconspiritor had said what was now claimed by the prosecution, Berkman asked, "Why wasn't she arrested on the spot?" Because, he went on, there was no conscription law on the books when she finished speaking at 9:45 that evening. Wilson didn't sign it until 10 p.m. Besides, many congressmen had been just as outspoken in their opposition to the draft as Goldman. No, the two were not on trial for "conspiracy"; they were on trial, Berkman concluded, "because we are anarchists."

If so, Goldman made certain that anarchism "raised its voice in an American court" for the first time since the Haymarket trial. From the outset, she was on the attack, accusing the marshal of trying to "make New York safe for democracy" by turning her office "into a battlefield," which resembled "invaded Belgium." She also read from the Declaration of Independence before placing herself in the company not only of Thomas Jefferson, but also of Patrick Henry, William Lloyd Garrison, John Brown, and Henry David Thoreau. Had they always operated within the law? No. Was she a criminal for defending draft evaders? Not in her eyes. Did her opposition to the draft make her any less a patriot? Not in her mind. Insisting that "real patriots" love their country "with open eyes," she refused to blind herself to America's faults. She, too, was a patriot, a "greater patriot than those who shoot off firecrackers," and a greater patriot than those who leap to their feet at the playing of the "Star-Spangled Banner." (During the trial a defiant Goldman had remained seated whenever strains of the anthem wafted into the courtroom, courtesy of a band outside a nearby recruiting station.)

The prosecutor chose not to challenge Goldman's patriotism directly. Instead, he reminded the jury that the "real Emma Goldman" was not in the courtroom. The "real" Goldman, he argued, could only be witnessed on the platform. "There she is in her true element. . . . There she inflames the young, [this] menace to our well-ordered institutions."

One of those institutions was working so smoothly that the presiding judge could afford to read copies of *Mother Earth* and Berkman's *Prison Memoirs* while he presided. When it came time for him to deliver his charge to the jury, Judge Julius Mayer was ready. Freedom of speech was not the issue in this trial, he intoned. "Free speech," he went on, "is guaranteed to us under the constitution. . . . But free speech means not license, not counseling disobedience." The only question to be decided was whether the defendants had "conspired" to violate the Selective Service Act. What constituted a conspiracy? Judge Mayer declared it "sufficient if two or more persons in any manner or through any contrivance should even tacitly come to a mutual understanding to accomplish a common and unlawful desire."

The jury soon proved to be an efficient machine of justice as well. Only thirty-nine minutes were required to find Goldman and Berkman guilty. Judge Mayer then levied the maximum penalty of two years in jail and a $10,000 find apiece before departing from his script to recommend deportation upon conclusion of their respective prison terms. Goldman's litany of great American lawbreakers notwithstanding, Judge Mayer's America was not a place "for those who express the view that the law may be disobeyed in accordance with the choice of the individual." With that, a subdued Berkman was ordered to the federal prison in Atlanta and an unrepentant Goldman was dispatched to the Missouri State Penitentiary in Jefferson City.

The two had barely arrived at their new homes when a friendly lawyer secured their temporary freedom. Though not an anarchist, Harry Weinberger had established himself as a vigorous defender of radicals and radical causes. Having once served as Goldman's attorney in a birth control case, he had offered his services to her prior to the conspiracy trial. Imagining this courtroom as her stage, she had declined. Now that the trial was over, Weinberger was determined to overturn the verdict. First he had to find a federal judge willing to free the two while their appeal was being argued. On July 20 newly appointed Supreme Court Justice Louis Brandeis signed the order that returned Goldman and Berkman to New York. Then Weinberger went to work challenging the constitutionality of the draft by arguing that the Selective Service Act violated the First and Thirteenth Amendments, as well as the constitutional ban against religious establishments (because the draft law did exempt some religious objectors).

While the courts began to ponder her fate, Goldman went immediately to Rochester on family business. Her sister Helena was distraught over her son's decision to enlist. A violinist without strong political views, David Hochstein thought that he had a duty to his country. Subsequently he fought in Europe, dying in the battle of the Argonne Forest just days before the war ended. His mother never recovered, dying a broken woman for whom Goldman alternately felt sadness (for Helena's loss) and contempt (for her inability to surmount it).

Goldman harbored similar emotions for Reitman. Before her trial, he had left for Chicago despite Goldman's request that he remain with her. Not surprised by his decision, Goldman was still "exasperated and pained" by his failure to stand by her. To make matters worse, she learned that he had tried to enlist in the medical corps. It was bad enough that the country had become a giant "lunatic asylum"; it was far worse that nephews and lovers had been drawn in by the "war mania."

Once again, Berkman came to Goldman's rescue, this time by occupying her time and mind as she waited to learn the court's decision. Upon his return to New York, Berkman was held in the Tombs Prison, having been jolted by one final aftershock from the San Francisco Preparedness Day explosion. California authorities demanded his extradition. Once back in New York, Goldman went to work organizing demonstrations. Russian friends even marched for Berkman in Moscow and St. Petersburg. Finally the San Francisco district attorney relented. There would be no trial, but not until November was Berkman released.

Mother Earth also demanded Goldman's attention. In August the Post Office Department banned it from the mails for violating the Espionage Act. With some help from Reitman,

Mother Earth's self-described "janitor," Goldman arranged to publish a briefer substitute called the *Mother Earth Bulletin.* However, his instinct for "caution" on the war issue strained relations between the two even further. "One day the storm broke and Ben left," this time "for good." And the *Bulletin?* The December issue was withheld from the mails because it contained a story concerning the hanging of thirteen "Negro soldiers" on a Texas army base. Four months later, it, too, was declared permanently "unmailable."

In Goldman's view, the contrast between American repression and Russian freedom was growing more striking by the day. If she would not go to Russia, she wanted to speak to Americans about liberation there. If she had to serve her jail sentence, she was anxious to use her freedom to speak against the war policies of the U.S. government. The same federal marshal who had arrested her in June tried to stop her from speaking publicly while the Supreme Court considered her appeal. In protest, Goldman went before audiences with a gag covering her mouth, until the attorney general intervened to permit her to return to the lecture circuit.

By this point, anarchists were far from alone in their opposition to the war. By late summer antiwar Wobblies and socialists were targeted for prosecution under the Espionage Act. The "American Hun," according to Goldman, was no longer discriminating between one radical group and another. Now their previous failure to support her was "coming back to haunt them." The "poor fools" had been silent when the "persecution" was directed solely against the anarchists. Now it was their turn to "pay the price" for their reluctance to challenge the "war hysteria" from the beginning.

Goldman was convinced that had more Americans, radical or otherwise, fought the decision for war immediately, U.S. troops might not be heading for Europe and she might not be facing a jail sentence. By August it was too late to stop the war machine, and her own fate was out of her hands. All she could do was hope that the expanded repression might eventually benefit the left by revealing the essential fraudulence of American democracy.

When Lenin came to power in Russia, Goldman returned briefly to the speaker's platform. This time her message shifted from the hypocrisy of American democracy to the possibilities of its Russian-bred variety. Viewing herself as an unofficial publicist for the Bolsheviks, she spoke in their defense, published pamphlets ("The Truth About the Bolsheviki"), and put her "love child" (the *Mother Earth Bulletin*) behind Lenin's revolution. Despite some disturbing signals, she held to her pro-Bolshevik line during the winter of 1917–1918. Kropotkin opposed the Bolsheviks, but his support for the Allies had already damaged his credibility in her eyes. Many American anarchists were skeptical of the Bolsheviks, and reports from anarchists in Russia told of Bolshevik raids against them. Still, Goldman refused to abandon the Bolsheviks. Their revolution was comparable to its American counterpart of 1776. Lenin and his followers were "libertarians," and the Russian people were "communistic" by nature. To her way of thinking, these last two categories were entirely compatible. The Bolsheviks were Marxists and, therefore, "governmentalists," but they believed what she believed—namely in the possibility of the immediate creation of a utopia where equality reigned.

Goldman's shift from liberty to confinement was sudden as well. Without a dissenting vote, the Supreme Court in early January upheld the constitutionality of the draft. On February 4, Goldman and Berkman surrendered as scheduled to New York authorities. The next day Goldman was once again behind bars. For the first time in her occasional career as an American prisoner, she found it difficult to accept her lot. Every day proved harder than the day before. She was nearly fifty. Recurring back problems and the onset of menopause took a physical and psychological toll. Continuing reports of both American and Soviet repression of dissenters added to her mental burdens. Even her "one great love"—her "ideal"— could not always be counted on to boost her spirits.

Goldman's daily schedule left her exhausted. Up at 5:30 a.m. to clean her cell and eat breakfast (in silence), she worked from 6:30 to 11:30, ate lunch (in silence), and returned to the shop from 12:30 to 4:30 before more "awful food" (in silence).

Her standing work assignment was to sew either fifty-four jackets or eighteen dozen suspenders under the daily supervision of a "miserable gutter-snipe of a twenty-one-year-old boy paid to get results." It was almost a return to her days with Leopold Garson. In America, Goldman may have gained fame and notoriety for being an anarchist, but her first and last jobs were as a lowly seamstress.

At least the shop, "terrible as it was," was an improvement over being locked in a cell. Double the size of the "pest-holes" Goldman occupied in 1893, these cells were poorly lit and more poorly ventilated. She thought she had an explanation for the latter: Southerners do "not care much for fresh air." She did, but not enough to go to church on Sunday. Apparently, only those who attended religious services were permitted a Sunday afternoon of outdoor exercise. Having rejected the first (because no one was able to tune or play the piano!), she was denied the second.

After the fact, Goldman could laugh about her final tour of prison duty. But at the time, she had all that she could do to survive each day, until she returned to her role as unofficial den mother to her sister inmates, including the black prisoners. This prison tour represented her first long-term contact with any American blacks. In a sense, it is somewhat ironic that publication of the *Mother Earth Bulletin* had been suspended for an article concerning black Americans, because the original *Mother Earth* seldom dealt with black issues, and Goldman's lectures attracted few black listeners. Nonetheless, she came to appreciate the "solidarity" of the black inmates, who may well have needed her less than she needed their example.

Goldman's closest comrades within the prison were the other political prisoners, though the warden denied that such a classification existed. Most prominent among the "politicals" was Kate Richards O'Hare, who arrived in April 1919. A Kansan by birth and a socialist by choice, O'Hare had been convicted of violating the Espionage Act. Initially, Goldman was put off by both O'Hare's hard-edged manner and her "childlike faith," a characteristic that Goldman found overabundant in native-born Americans. On the outside, the two women no doubt would have engaged in bitter arguments, for O'Hare was a dogmatic socialist who believed in obtaining power via the ballot box and using that power to build a centralized state. Inside the prison, however, they were comrades, who employed whatever persuasive skills they could muster to improve everything from the food (hotter) to the paint (whiter).

O'Hare was more generous and earthier in her praise of Goldman: "Emma don't believe in Jesus, yet she is the one who makes it possible for me to grasp the spirit of Jesus." Why? Because she put herself at the service of others. The women inmates "didn't know if anarchy was a breakfast food or a corn cure; but Emma *did* things for them." For Goldman, in or out of prison, motherhood continued to be her mission. To O'Hare, Goldman in prison was the "tender, cosmic mother."

She was also the resident short-order cook. Gourmet cooking was her "great vice." In her New York apartments, she prepared many a lecture over her stove. In prison she was reduced to making bad coffee, concocting strange sandwiches, and boiling eggs. Distributing her handiwork taught her the "real meaning of crookedness." The prison bars were very close together, but gradually the women learned to pass food through them "by all sorts of contortionist motions."

Goldman took pride in her prison cooking, but friends worried that she was becoming too much of a woman. Her letters contained repeated requests for stockings and nightgowns, hardly the trappings of the devoted revolutionary. Finally, their responses brought a confession: "I always was more feminine than is good for a dyed-in-the-blood revolutionist."

When it came to Russia, Goldman still regarded herself as a "revolutionist," even at the risk of breaking with the woman she called the "mother of us all." Catherine Breshkovskaya had long been Goldman's idol. A force behind the 1905 Russian revolution, Breshkovskaya had briefly supported the Bolsheviks before turning completely against them. To Goldman, her attacks on the Bolsheviks constituted a "fearful shock." In correspondence with Breshkovskaya, Goldman urged her not to align herself with the "white generals and Jew-baiters" of Russia. She pleaded with Breshkovskaya to hold her criticisms so long as "every government is at the throat of the Bolsheviks." Not only did her "'mother" reject Goldman's advice, but Breshkovskaya predicted that her ideological daughter would one day be on her side. From prison, Goldman "scorned" the suggestion and ceased all correspondence with Breshkovskaya, signing off her last letter, "your heartbroken child, Emma."

In the meantime, Goldman was preoccupied with the mounting evidence of repression in America. Until the November armistice, both the Espionage Act and the Sedition Act provided a regular supply of defendants for American courtrooms. Bill Haywood and Gene Debs were among hundreds of new convicts. Surveillance was an ongoing reality. Letters between Goldman and Berkman were regularly intercepted and read. Within a year of its demise, virtually all 8,000 *Mother Earth* subscribers had made it into the files of military intelligence. Within the Justice Department of Attorney General A. Mitchell Palmer, plans for the deportation of alien radicals went forward. Card files on suspected "reds" reached 60,000 by the fall of 1919. With Germany defeated, a new, but related, threat had emerged. The "hun" and the "red" would seem to be disparate species, but in the supercharged atmosphere of 1919 they were not.

Strikes rocked the country. Letter bombs meant for prominent politicians and businessmen were discovered, and other bombs actually exploded, one on the front steps of the home of Attorney General Palmer. Some 5 million copies of Lenin's "Letter to the American Worker" were distributed across the country. At least fifty Bolshevik-inspired publications were in circulation. There had to be an explanation for all this, or at least a scapegoat. And "reds" were conveniently available. There were reds in the immigrant-dominated Communist Party of America. There were more reds in the rival Communist Labor Party, led by radical journalist John Reed, who had testified for Goldman at her 1917 trial. There were reds behind the strikes and the bombs. And there were reds, a senate committee was told, who could be traced to the "revolutionary socialism" of Germany.

A member of that same senate committee, Senator Miles Poindexter of Washington, wondered publicly why one of those reds was not a candidate for immediate deportation. In fact, when Poindexter put that very question directly to Palmer, the individual in question had just been released from prison four months early for "good behavior."

On September 28, Goldman left the Missouri State Penitentiary. Her first destination was Chicago to see Reitman, his new wife and son. "The dead had buried the dead," she later wrote, "and I was serene." Then she went to Rochester to see Helena and their mother for what proved to be the last time. All the while she remained under the watchful eye of what she called the Department of "In-Justice." One of its agents had actually hired on as Goldman's personal secretary. In addition, Judge Mayer's deportation order was still in force. Senator Poindexter remained concerned, and Attorney General Palmer remained in need of scapegoats. As a result, Goldman's freedom was short-lived indeed.

On October 17, the Senate passed a resolution asking the attorney general to inform that body if he had taken action against Goldman and other alien radicals and "if not, why not." Their patience was wearing thin. After all, the woman was out of jail and back on the platform, attacking prison conditions in America, praising the Bolsheviks in Russia, and thundering against her enemies and the enemies of liberty everywhere.

Those enemies, Goldman soon discovered, included Attorney General Palmer and an eager Justice Department bureaucrat named J. Edgar Hoover. Shortly after passage of the senate resolution, Palmer personally issued a warrant for her arrest under the Alien Immigration Act of 1917, which called for the deportation of undesirable aliens "any time after their entry," and the Anti-Anarchist Act of 1918. On the heels of the arrest came a Justice Department report on its investigation of radicals. Fully half of the document dealt with "Exhibit 6" (Goldman), which included everything from her 1893 trial to the McKinley assassination to the July 1914 issue of *Mother Earth*. The individual responsible for the report was Hoover, who was determined to remove from the country two of its "most dangerous anarchists"—Goldman and Berkman.

On October 27, Goldman appeared before a panel charged with determining her status under the two laws in question. Meanwhile, Berkman had waived all his appeals, declaring himself ready to return to Russia. Goldman was prepared to join him, but she wanted to see the process out. Just prior to the hearing, a *Mother Earth* associate offered to marry her in order to establish her American citizenship. On Weinberger's advice, she declined. Apparently, both mistakenly thought she could still claim citizenship through her marriage to Kersner.

Weinberger did make an impassioned plea at her hearing. After quoting Jefferson on the virtues of liberty and tolerance, he argued that the law dictated tolerance for his client: Goldman was not an anarchist when she had arrived in 1885; therefore, she could not be deported for subsequently becoming an anarchist.

Goldman sat silently throughout the hearing. But she did submit a written statement blasting the "star chamber proceedings" that she had been forced to undergo:

> If the present proceedings are for the purpose of proving some alleged offense committed by me . . . then I protest against the secrecy and third degree methods. . . . But if I am not charged with any specific offense . . . then I protest still more vigorously against these proceedings.

Goldman argued that the "real purpose" behind wartime repression and her deportation was the maintenance of the "capitalist status quo." A month later she was ordered out of the United States. On November 29, 1919, Assistant Labor Secretary Louis Post signed her deportation documents. Years earlier Post had worked with Goldman to secure the release of John Turner. On the day he affixed his signature to her deportation order he condemned the "Know-Nothing Immigration Laws." But he signed the necessary papers, and Goldman never forgave him for doing so.

With her time running out, Goldman decided to undertake one more impromptu lecture tour. This, she feared, was her "last opportunity to raise my voice against the shame of my adopted land." There would be appeals in the interim, but she had little reason for optimism. So off she went on a series of farewell speeches. Included on her itinerary was Chicago, where she learned of the death of Henry Clay Frick. On December 5 she reported to Ellis Island. A week later she waived her final Supreme Court appeal from her makeshift cell. Berkman was ready to go, and now she was ready to join him. All that remained was a trip to the dentist, a few farewell visits, and one last request of Reitman: "Keep my memory alive." Then there was nothing left to do except sit and wait, confined to "the worst dump I ever stayed in."

CHAPTER NINE

At Sea

❖
❖

Ellis Island. Immigrants of all creeds, tongues, and hues approached this plot of land with great anticipation and even greater uncertainty. Interrogators awaited them, and queries asked and answered would determine their immediate fate. From this small island, these anxious arrivals would either be returned to their country of origin or funneled into the United States. But on the night of December 20, 1919, Ellis Island was the scene of a very different drama. On this cold Saturday night the island was a temporary home for 249 detainees, whose answers had always proved wanting and whose fate had already been decided.

All 249 were alien radicals who had been living in the United States. Since none was formally a citizen of the United States, all were eligible for their impending journey. Among their number were three women, the most famous of whom was Emma Goldman.

Goldman's public face indicated that she was ready, even anxious, to begin her life in exile. So what if a scornful America had spurned her? Mother Russia awaited her. Buoyed by her faith in the November Revolution, she was prepared to tell the world that she was proud and happy to be going home.

But privately Goldman fretted over being removed from the country that had been her home for better than two-thirds of her life. Now fifty, she had grown accustomed to a life of struggle, controversy, and celebrityhood in America. So, on her final night on American soil, she dressed entirely in black and confided to a friend that she felt as if "my insides [had been] pulled out of me."

None of the 249 had been informed of the specific timetable for their departure, leaving Goldman and her compatriots with little to do but wait and sleep—and wait some more. At two o'clock Sunday morning the wait was over. Goldman was awakened just as a Coast Guard cutter carrying congressmen, government officials, and J. Edgar Hoover approached Ellis Island. At about the same time a transport ship of Spanish-American War vintage was moving through drifting ice to its rendezvous point on the tip of Staten Island. This was the *Buford*, soon to be home for Goldman and her comrades as they headed across the Atlantic.

At 3:00 a.m. the deportees marched single file to a wait-. ing army tender, manned by soldiers with fixed bayonets. The walk was a brief one, but with reporters afoot, Goldman managed to proclaim her joy at being dispatched to Russia— and to predict her triumphal return to the United States—before she disappeared into the bowels of the tender.

Within the hour, the crowded tender was headed on a course that took it just past the Statue of Liberty to its meeting with the *Buford*. Goldman was struck by the irony of it all. Thirty-four Decembers earlier she had thrilled at the sight of the lady and her torch. Only weeks before, "Miss Liberty" had been set on her pedestal, making a sixteen-year-old Goldman among the first to pass under her raised arm. But in the murky predawn hours of this December day in 1919, Goldman could only gaze cynically at this empty symbol of liberty and dream of "breathing free" somewhere other than in the United States.

The transfer to the *Buford* was carried out with cold efficiency, but not in total silence. As Goldman boarded the aging ship, one of the congressmen could not resist a derisive "Merry Christmas, Emma!" His greeting drew a thumbed nose from the Jewish atheist, whose failure to speak did not necessarily mean that she was at a loss for words. At that moment the public and private Emma Goldman were one. There she was, standing on the gangplank of the ship, glaring down at those who had hounded her out of the country before signaling her final gesture of defiance.

Before the sun was up, this first of a projected series of "Soviet Arks" was at sea. In a sense, one of its most famous passengers would remain in a similar state for the rest of her life.

For Hoover, it was crucial that both Goldman and Berkman were on the maiden "ark." Hoover's goal was not simply to rid the United States of two notorious anarchists, but to garner public support for new legislation aimed at limiting dissent within the United States. The mysteries surrounding the departure of the *Buford* and the armed soldiers guarding the deportees were both parts of the same piece. Hoover, too, knew a good dramatic opportunity when he saw one. Just in case anyone questioned the legitimacy of the government's actions, these extraordinary precautions ought to be proof positive that Goldman and Berkman really were dangerous characters. If any doubts still persisted, the Justice Department chose the day of the *Buford*'s departure to release a report alleging their involvement in "nearly a score" of killings and assassinations.

Not to be outdone, Goldman and Berkman produced a pamphlet of their own, "Deportation: Its Meaning and Menace," as their contribution to a U.S. propaganda war that threatened to live on long after they were gone. Writing at odd moments while on Ellis Island, the two dwelt on the antiwar hysteria of 1917–1918. Few enemies, including Hoover, escaped their wrath, but their real targets were liberal, and even radical, intellectuals who supported President Wilson's war and the suppression of civil liberties that accompanied it. Placing themselves once again in the individualist tradition of Jefferson, they took time to fire this final shot across their bow before climbing aboard the *Buford*. Along with it came an implicit warning (America could ill afford enforced Americanism) and an open plea (Americans ought to return to their sacred roots).

En route, however, Goldman had more immediate worries, including the behavior of her military guard, the *Buford*'s seaworthiness, and the danger of striking unretrieved mines. None of these fears turned out to be worth the time invested in them. On January 16 the *Buford* docked safely at Hango, Finland. Three days later Goldman and Berkman reached the Russian border, where they were greeted by a delegation of Soviet authorities. Now it was time to worry about her ability to "work within the limited confines of the state—Bolshevist or otherwise."

During the ensuing two years, "Red Emma" would discover that Red Russia was not her ideological home. She had spent years in the service of her revolutionary dreams and had longed for the day when revolution would liberate the oppressed. She had rhapsodized about the cleansing power of revolution, but when faced with the fact of revolution, she often looked the other way. When confronted with the demands of revolution, she eventually opted out.

Initially, however, both Goldman and Berkman were willing to accept the regime's official line, which explained all repression as the necessary response to external dangers. Of course, the Bolsheviks did face great dangers and real enemies. Allied armies had only recently withdrawn from Russia, and an allied naval blockade remained in force. Victory in a civil war against "counterrevolutionaries," from monarchists to liberals, had yet to be won. Harsh centralization was "absolutely necessary," Goldman conceded, if the revolution was to survive. She accepted this line of reasoning with minimal reservations in her first weeks in the womb of the revolution. But soon feelings of "disillusionment" and utter betrayal took hold of her. Once they did, neither ever let go.

Right from the outset there were ominous hints of things to come. En route from the Russo-Finnish border to Petrograd (formerly St. Petersburg), Goldman rode in the same rail compartment with her host, a party functionary named Zorin, who had lived for a time in the United States. She was relieved to be able to converse in English, but she was not pleased to hear what Zorin had to say. The Party, he enthused, compared favorably to New York's Tammany Hall machine. Goldman offered no response to this "discordant note." A few days later Zorin informed her that "free speech" was nothing more than a "bourgeois superstition." Goldman readied a protest but held back, thinking that she had no right to judge "this nascent revolution." Still, her first days in Petrograd were far from reassuring. Freedom in all its forms was at the heart of her understanding of anarchism. Freedom denied was no way to begin an experiment in revolution.

Goldman remembered old St. Petersburg as a city "full of life and mystery." Not so the Petrograd of 1920, where people "walked about like living corpses," goaded by the "search for a piece of bread or a stick of wood." The "utter stillness" of it all was "paralyzing."

On some days only the sound of gunfire broke the "awful, oppressive silence." Was civil war that close? Were executions? No, Goldman told herself. Zorin had made it clear that capital punishment had been abolished. Besides, this was not the time for entertaining doubts. The revolution was still young, and she had "come to learn."

Goldman's impromptu teachers were the famous and the ordinary. John Reed, an old friend from her Greenwich Village days, was in Petrograd. Bolshevik sympathizer and author of an instant history of the revolution, *Ten Days That Shook the World*, Reed told her that the "dark side" of the regime was a temporary phenomenon. Her search for some confirmation of Reed's optimism brought her to the Petrograd apartment of Maxim Gorky. Surely this writer, who, by his pen alone, had made the "social outcast our kin," would be able to reassure his visitor that all was right with the revolution. Not so. Goldman left her first meeting with a tired and distracted Gorky feeling empty and depressed. A second, purely accidental meeting aboard a train bound for Moscow produced a confrontation initiated by an angry Goldman. Had he really called for prison terms for what he called "morally defective" children? Yes, replied the startled writer; "moral defection" was spreading among the young, and the state had an obligation to counter the "disease" by isolating those who carried it.

More distressing was Goldman's own awareness that the revolution had not eliminated basic inequalities. Instead, they had simply been rearranged so that Communist Party members now ranked as the first among equals. Goldman learned this truth daily in the kitchen of the Hotel Astoria. Food was obviously in short supply, and rationing was necessary. All this she accepted as an inevitable side effect of war, revolution, and the Allied blockade. What she could not accept was preferential treatment for Party members quartered in the Astoria.

One day, while Goldman was waiting her turn in a food line, a young girl barged in front to demand vinegar. Immediately a number of other women responded in chorus: Just who was she to insist upon what was clearly a luxury? The "servant" of a high Party official, came the reply. What right did that give her to issue demands? answered one. He was her "master," the girl informed her challenger. Besides, he was a "hard-working" master who deserved this small bonus. Instantly a "storm of indignation broke loose." Wasn't the purpose of the revolution to do away with masters and servants, both of whom were creatures of the past?

Goldman was shaken, but she was also impressed with the behavior of her line mates. These women had an "instinctive" sense of justice. They saw inequality "at every step, and they bitterly resented it." This was a hopeful sign to an anarchist who had found little reason for optimism in revolutionary Petrograd. Perhaps Moscow would be better.

Though feeling "torn in a hundred directions" in Petrograd, Goldman and Berkman intended to establish residence there. It was a cosmopolitan city, a Western city, and the "'revolutionary workers' center." Moscow was the seat of government; therefore, these anarchists preferred to be "far distant" from it. A brief visit, they trusted, would not contaminate them.

Moscow, Reed had warned her, was a "military encampment" laced with spies. Secret police were nowhere and everywhere. Goldman had to see for herself. What struck her immediately was the bustle of the city. Compared to the "desert" that was Petrograd, the streets of Moscow were alive with people. It did not take her long to discover that soldiers and secret police were everywhere. Moreover, Muscovites "seemed to have no common interest between them." Life in Moscow was too much like life in New York: "Everyone rushed about as a detached unit in quest of his own, pushing and knocking against everyone else."

Among these Muscovites was Angelica Balabanova, Communist Party member and secretary of the Third Internationale. Goldman knew of her, and after listening to Reed and Gorky defend the revolution, she was anxious to get a woman's point of view. Balabanova was a pleasant surprise, precisely because she avoided the "usual excuses." Yes, there was a scarcity of food and fuel, but the villain was not solely the blockade. Russian life was simply "mean and limited."

While in Moscow, Goldman learned of the "Black Guards," armed anarchists who specialized in robberies and other terrorist acts. During her first weeks in Russia, she had deliberately kept her distance from other anarchists, whether prone to violence or not. She knew of their opposition to the growing centralization of Lenin's regime, and she had been told that anarchists had become targets of Bolshevik machine-gun fire. At the very least their newspapers had been shut down and their printing presses had been confiscated. Gradually, Goldman did establish contact with a few anarchists, including Kropotkin, who had returned there to live—and to conclude that Bolshevism was a "conspiracy" against the dream of revolution and equality.

Troubled, but still withholding judgment, Goldman decided to go directly to Lenin. She had read his pamphlet, "State and Revolution," which she decided was an anarchist's manifesto. "So long as the state exists there is no freedom," he wrote. "When there is freedom, there will be no state." How could the author of those words order the execution of anarchists, or even act to suppress their words?

When Goldman was ushered into the great man's presence, she found Lenin holding a copy of *The Trial and Speeches of Alexander Berkman and Emma Goldman*. Before she could acknowledge his gesture, Lenin the propagandist praised Goldman the propagandist: "It is worth going to prison if the courts can so successfully be turned into a forum."

Goldman had to have been pleased, but she soon felt Lenin's "stead cold gaze upon me, penetrating my very being."

Speaking in Russian, he asked her when revolution could be expected in the United States. She had been asked similar questions many times before, but she was "astounded" to hear these words coming from Lenin. How could this man know so little about life in America? Why, Wilson's administration had imprisoned many revolutionaries, and not a few were in the process of being expelled. She was a living witness to its draconian activities. Furthermore, she was not standing across from Lenin to receive her revolutionary marching orders for America, but to keep the Russian revolution on a course she deemed proper.

When Lenin asked Goldman what she wanted to do for the revolution in Russia, she called for the creation of a Russian society to promote freedom in America. After all, Americans had done as much for Russia prior to 1917. Now it was Russia's turn to rescue America. Lenin "appeared enthusiastic," but he cautioned that any Goldman-inspired organization would have to operate under the auspices of the Third Internationale.

Now Goldman saw an opportunity to broach the subject that had prompted her to see Lenin in the first place: Never could she think of working for the Soviets in any capacity as long as her anarchist comrades were in prison "for opinion's sake." Literally "scores" of anarchists were being held in Soviet jails, she reminded Lenin. What was their crime? Speaking their minds?

"There can be no free speech in a revolutionary period," shrugged Lenin.

Goldman conceded that Russia was in the middle of a "revolutionary period," but not since Homestead had she believed that the end justified any means necessary to obtain it. In recent months she had been the victim of another government's conviction that the end (a successful prosecution of a war) justified the means (suppression of wartime dissent). No bourgeois woman herself, Goldman was not ready to concede that freedom of speech was simply a bourgeois invention. To her it was one of the "spiritual achievements of centuries," but one that apparently meant nothing to this "puritan" in her presence.

Lenin was certain that "his scheme alone would redeem Russia." Those who disagreed, whether violently or nonviolently, were not to be tolerated. "A shrewd Asiatic" this puritan was. Goldman left his presence unawed—and convinced that his approach to people was quite the same as his approach to both revolution and the wielding of revolutionary power—that is to say, "purely utilitarian."

Goldman returned to Petrograd in time for May Day. Thirty years earlier this international holiday for all workers had been observed for the first time in the United States, and she had been among the celebrants in the streets of New York City. Over the intervening years May Day had remained an "inspiring event." She could only then dream of observing May Day in a "free country." Now she was about to have that chance—or so she anticipated on the morning of May 1, 1920.

The city was awash in a sea of red banners, and crowds had gathered early for the parades and pageantry. Goldman had been offered a place on the reviewing stand, but she declined, preferring instead to mingle among the people on her first May Day in a "free country." Instead of singing and spontaneous laughter, however, she experienced only silence and mechanistic routine. Obviously disappointed, she attributed the sullenness surrounding her to the failures of the revolution and its leaders, to the current custodians of her revolutionary ideal, not to civil war or to an Allied blockade.

The fact that the people of Petrograd were not dancing in the streets on that May Day was sad enough to Goldman, but that she wanted to dance, indeed, had *expected* to dance, made her day an even sadder one. After all, it was a younger, more exuberant Goldman who had once informed her friends and enemies alike that, if she couldn't dance, she wanted no part in their revolution.

Despite what she had observed, Goldman was not ready to abandon Lenin's version of her ideal. A Soviet Russia was not yet happy and free, but it could still be made so. She could still be part of this revolutionary process, if only she could find a task distant enough from the formal entanglements of government.

Despite her disappointments, Goldman did not want to leave Russia. Committed to the Russian people, if not to their leaders, she remained determined to find meaningful work. To her that meant work of a "nonpartisan character," work that would enable her to study economic and social conditions in Russia, and work that placed her in "direct touch" with ordinary people. The Museum of the Revolution, housed within the Winter Palace in Petrograd, proved to be her answer. Its director, who was pro-Bolshevik, but not a Party member, asked her to spend at least the summer of 1920 traveling in the Ukraine and the Caucasus gathering archival material relating to the revolution. Goldman had hoped to play a more "vital" role in Russia society, but she signed on nonetheless. In fact, she agreed to serve as the expedition's combined treasurer, housekeeper, and cook.

Officially, Berkman was to lead the group, which consisted of four others, including a communist student at the University of Petrograd. Together the six had to procure, paint, and outfit a railroad car, which they dubbed the Maxim Gorky. For the chief cook and housekeeper, the outfitting led to an afternoon of scouring the Winter Palace for china. Finally, on June 30, 1920, everything was in place, including the "borrowed" china. Goldman and her five compatriots were ready to set out on their historical hunt for the lost revolution. But the Maxim Gorky sat in Moscow for two weeks while the regime's bureaucracy churned out its final approval.

The delay gave Goldman an opportunity to visit once again with Peter Kropotkin. These two anarchists had had their differences over the years, but Goldman deeply respected Kropotkin and the unpretentious life he lived. In his cramped study, Goldman laid bare her doubts about the "ghastly reality" of the revolution. Was all the "terrorism," all the "agony" necessary? Kropotkin listened carefully to these lamentations before replying. When he finally did, he tried to boost her sagging spirits: What she had seen during her six months in Russia was only the surface of things. Beneath the "blunders" of the Party was a revolution that had penetrated the "soul of Russia." According to her mentor, there was no reason to lose faith just yet. The people were stronger than the Party. Without their direct participation, the Party was doomed to fail. "We anarchists," Kropotkin argued, "must be ready to pick up the pieces, to build local cooperatives, to do the hard work necessary to recapture the . . . revolution."

Encouraged by what she heard, Goldman left Kropotkin to rejoin the museum caravan bound for the Ukraine. However, neither the trip nor its mission proved sufficient to sustain her. In the Ukraine she was confronted with the anti-Semitism of the local peasants and the anti-Bolshevism of the Ukrainian Jews. For the first time in her life, Goldman had to concede that there was a "Jewish question" apart from any issue of class. Her own identification as a Jew had always been secular rather than religious. But in the Ukraine anti-Semitism was rampant. Pogroms remained an ongoing reality. No longer could she believe that Jewish emancipation would automatically accompany social revolution. Moreover, she concluded that the despised Bolshevik regime was virtually alone in trying to reduce anti-Jewish behavior in that region of Russia. What irony! Emma Goldman, anarchist, had to commend a powerful centralized state for its efforts to "check" anti-Semitism.

When faced with the ultimate choice of either identifying with the regime or retreating to her own private world, Goldman opted for the latter. Even while on the road for the museum, much of her time was spent writing letters to family and friends in the United States. In them, she made clear that her first desire was to return to America, that she could not escape feeling as though she was a "stranger in a strange land," that her work for the revolution, such as it was, was utterly "useless." Whether standing in line for food at the Astoria or riding a train through the Russian countryside, Goldman always saw herself as an outsider. Moreover, she realized that she needed time simply to adjust to daily life in what would have been a difficult land for her in ordinary times.

Goldman's association with the museum persisted through the fall. Not until late December did she return to Petrograd and to what she still assumed would be her Russian home for the foreseeable future. There she and Berkman set up house-keeping in the Hotel Astoria. Exhausted by their travels, they prepared to live quietly while they waited for the revolution to exhaust itself. As matters developed, they did not have to wait very long at all.

By February 1921, the two were witnesses to massive popular demands for an end to what Lenin called War Communism. Spontaneous strikes paralyzed the city and a populace already weakened by hunger. Strikers demanded an increase in food rations, the right to barter openly for food, and the elimination of road blocks that separated the city from the countryside—and from food. Such basic demands rapidly escalated to a full political agenda that called for granting civil and political liberties, including free speech and a free press.

The Petrograd Soviet responded to this challenge with a combination of minimal concessions and military force. These tactics brought an end to the strikes everywhere in the immediate vicinity, save among the sailors of the Kronstadt naval base. Located some twenty miles west of the city on an island in the Gulf of Finland, the base contained many supporters of the November revolution. Now they, too, wanted a more democratic Russia—and a more plentiful one as well. Hence their decision to endorse the demands of the Petrograd strikers and to arrest Bolshevik authorities on the base.

From their quarters, Goldman and Berkman were beset by conflicting emotions. Though in sympathy with the sailors, they (especially Berkman) had reservations about the rebels' emphasis on "bourgeois liberties." Though gratified by the sailors' "splendid solidarity" with the Petrograd workers, they worried that the regime would summarily act to crush the rebellion.

Out of their concerns grew daily meetings with fellow anarchists and a proposal that the two of them mediate the conflict between the sailors and the regime. (Unlike Goldman, Berkman had maintained fairly close relations with local Party officials.) Therefore, on the night of March 5, a committee of four anarchists (including Goldman and Berkman) drew up their offer of mediation. What the proposal lacked in specifics, it made up for in emotion: "Comrades Bolshevik, bethink your-selves before it is too late. Do not play with fire. . . ." Listen instead to the sailors. Let them "air their grievances in the open."

Two days later this appeal brought a reply of sorts. On March 7, Kronstadt came under military assault. For eleven days the bombardment continued. For eleven days Goldman listened to the sounds of war. For eleven days she was beside herself with grief (for the sailors), anger (at the regime), and contempt (for all those, Communist and non-Communist alike, who failed to protest this official violence).

Those eleven days sealed the immediate fate of the sailors and forever solidified Goldman's judgment of the regime that she had once embraced. Kronstadt came to symbolize all that had gone wrong with the revolution. All of her reservations had been confirmed at least elevenfold. Kronstadt crystallized her "disillusionment" with Bolshevism and the regime's betrayal of her. Kronstadt meant that she would have to leave Russia.

Goldman's departure from Russia, though certain in her mind, was not immediately obtainable. First Berkman had to be convinced. Then official approval had to be procured. In the meantime, the two moved to Moscow. The memory of Kronstadt was too immediate and too painful for them to re-main in Petrograd. Weeks stretched into months as the two lived a subdued life on the few U.S. dollars they had left. They entertained visiting anarchists and argued with those who still had kind words for the regime. Meanwhile, they waited for the only act of kindness they now wanted from the Soviet government: permission to leave.

Thanks to the intervention of Angelica Balabanova, Gold-man and Berkman were given Soviet passports sometime in late November 1921. A week later they crossed the Russian border into Latvia, consigned to a new life as exiles twice re-moved and convinced that it would "not be easy to go away."

Formally deported from the United States and informally dismissed by the Soviets, Goldman was officially—and ideo-logically—homeless as of January 1922. The first of a number of temporary havens was Stockholm, where she stayed just long enough to resolve any lingering doubts over whether she would reveal the "terrors" of Bolshevism to the rest of the world. Always in need of an audience, she had little difficulty persuading herself that she had a message of Bolshevik betrayal that the political left at least ought to hear.

Many of her friends on the left worried that Goldman's words would be used by their right-wing enemies to discredit all revolutions, all utopian possibilities, in fact all progressive social change. Despite this objection, and despite her respect for some of those who made it, Goldman plunged ahead anyway. An evil so monstrous had to be exposed and exorcised.

Once she found lodging in Stockholm, Goldman wasted little time in setting up shop as an anti-Bolshevik publicist. Her primary goal was to place articles in the American liberal press. Firm rejections greeted every overture. Her remaining choice was to confine herself to the small anarchist press or accept pending offers from "capitalist" publications. Over Berkman's heated objections, she agreed to sell her story. After anti-Bolshevik articles began to appear under the Goldman byline, the socialist prime minister of Sweden strongly hinted that she would have to find another home, since his government was on the verge of establishing diplomatic relations with Lenin's regime.

Through the intervention of anarchist friends, Goldman obtained a German visa and moved to Berlin. In her small apartment, she resumed a Stockholm affair with Arthur Swenson, a Swede twenty years her junior, and began to write a book on her two years in Russia. Swenson brought a brief period of happiness to a distracted and disoriented Goldman. Full of passion for her and her politics, he had pleaded with her to let him join her in Berlin. Although fearing the worst, she consented. Within a matter of months his ardor for her had cooled sufficiently that he returned to Sweden.

Goldman's book, which she had blandly titled *My Two Years in Russia,* chronicled her own fleeting affair with Bolshevism. Much to her chagrin, the publisher changed the title to *My Disillusionment in Russia* before lopping off the last twelve chapters. Goldman was livid, because the title implied that she rejected both Bolshevik misrule and the 1917 revolution at a time when she was still clinging to a distinction between the two. (The final dozen chapters were eventually published separately as *My Further Disillusionment in Russia*, thereby compounding her original grievance.)

Still, Goldman's analysis was enough to anger local German Communists, several hundred of whom disrupted a Berlin meeting she had organized to support Bolshevik-held political prisoners. She expected as much from true believers, but she was taken aback by the German government's call for her immediate departure. As of 1923, Bolshevism and Prussianism were searching for common ground. Goldman in Berlin was an unwelcome presence as their tentative dance grew more intimate. A stateless pawn in the hands of forces and regimes with more power than she could muster in her defense, she was forced to find yet another new home. This nonbeliever in the beneficence of any state power found herself once again at the mercy of any state friendly enough—and confident enough—to take her in.

If truth be told, Goldman had come to dislike the "German atmosphere." In a very real sense, both Moscow and Washington felt less oppressive to her than did Berlin in 1923. Ignored by the liberals, attacked by the communists, berated by the government, she knew she would have to leave. But where would she go? London was a possibility. So, feeling very much like a "released prisoner," Goldman arrived for a visit during which she planned to scout for a new home and proselytize among the non-Communist British left.

By this point in her intellectual odyssey, Goldman was ready to concede that the evils of Leninism were, in fact, implicit in Bolshevik ideology itself. The repression, the terror, the suffering, the starvation, the lofty position of Party members and the lowly status of the masses were not due to the Allied blockade, to civil war, or even to Leninist excesses. Instead, all were directly traceable to the ideology of the revolution itself. The last step had been taken. The last bridge had been burned. By 1924, Goldman, though still a woman of the left, was an anti-Bolshevik without apology or escape.

For better than eight months Goldman lived in London, recruiting allies, badgering the hesitant, and lamenting her failures. These eight months brought her into heady contact with many leading Western intellectuals, but they were also months of self-described "disastrous defeat."

Shortly after Goldman's arrival in London, the English novelist Rebecca West arranged a dinner in her honor. Better than 250 intellectuals, including H. G. Wells, Havelock Ellis, and Bertrand Russell, gathered to honor to Goldman before settling back in their chairs to listen to her acceptance of their plaudits. What she had to say caused some to tumble backward in those chairs and others to bolt from them in protest: Why reject the Bolsheviks? Why spurn your own past? Why cast your lot with conservatives whose hatred of Bolshevism colors everything they see?

Russell, for one, informed Goldman that he could not join her, despite his great personal affection for her. He agreed that Lenin's regime was drastically off course, but he was "not prepared to advocate any alternative government" for Russia. Moreover, he did not believe that anarchism was a realistic possibility anywhere: "The abolition of all government [will not be achieved] during the twentieth century."

Goldman responded by cutting off all correspondence with the philosopher. Not so with her old friend Roger Baldwin. Like Russell, Baldwin was a target of Goldman's overtures during the 1920s. Unlike Russell, Baldwin continued to be a part of Goldman's circle long after their serious differences over the Soviet Union were obvious to both of them. At times Goldman sought the civil libertarian's assistance in rescuing political prisoners from Soviet jails. At other times she wanted to enlist him in her campaign against American "liberals" (including Baldwin himself) who had remained silent in the face of Lenin's violations of civil liberties: "These people who shouted themselves hoarse for amnesty of political prisoners, how dare they keep silent now that their own pet government is guilty of such heinous crimes." Preferring to stress Soviet Russia's economic (as opposed to strictly political) democracy, Baldwin refused to be silent—or to agree with Goldman.

Daily life in England had not helped Goldman's general frame of mind either. The English were "hypocritical, cold, self-centered, and drab." Intellectuals aside, Goldman had exhausted her faith in the English working class and was unable to establish any links with the English middle class, whose "shopkeeper tendencies" made them indifferent to "life's deepest tragedies." To talk of a potential anarchist revolution to the masses of English office and factory workers was utterly pointless: "I should prefer talking to a mummy."

Goldman left England in the summer of 1925 with only one tangible accomplishment: a British passport. James Colton, a Welch coal miner and an anarchist, had agreed to marry her so that she might at least have this single benefit of citizenship. The double failure of her marriages to Jacob Kersner had long ago convinced Goldman that this institution was not for her. Marriage to James Colton was not evidence that she had changed her mind.

Love, however, was another matter entirely. Love without marriage Goldman had experienced many times in her life. Love she continued to hope might be hers yet again. Still, she knew, and feared, that reality was closing in on her. Nearing sixty, she was an "emancipated woman" alone in the world. Swenson had long since returned to Sweden, never to be heard from again. Berkman was still a part of her life, but by this point he had his own life in Berlin and a very young girl named Emmy Eckstein to live it with him.

The unfairness of it all did not escape Goldman. Why did society frown on relationships between older women and younger men and yet smile on men who remained attractive to younger women? When it came to questions such as these, Goldman was not above revealing her bitterness. Nor was she beyond directing her feelings at Berkman himself. Comrades in absentia, they were still able to confide in one another and were still searching for love and happiness in a world too conventional to accept their definitions of either.

On this score, Goldman could not help but be aware of the differences in their circumstances. Berkman had Eckstein to minister to him, to dote on him, while she had no one to share her joys or her tears with. As she approached sixty, Goldman was trying—with great difficulty—to come to terms with problems faced by older, unmarried, heterosexual, modern women. No matter how modern the older woman, Goldman lamented to Berkman, she could not avoid the pain that accompanied the absence of a home and family. She had always prided herself on being that modern woman. Now she could only see "tragedy" where previously she had found opportunity. Now she could not help but conclude that even anarchists needed that one other "who really cares." At various times in her life, Goldman had had the comfort of someone else who cared. But not now, and maybe never again.

The latter half of the 1920s produced few happy moments for Goldman. In 1927 her travels took her to Canada, where she found "no inspiration," owing to its depressing similarity to England and to her tantalizing proximity to the United States. The latter was especially agonizing, because during her Canadian tour the state of Massachusetts finally carried out the executions of immigrant anarchists Nicola Sacco and Bartolomeo Vanzetti. Arrested and convicted for the robbery and murder of a payroll guard in 1920, Sacco and Vanzetti had become international symbols of the anarchist-as-victim. As the day of their scheduled execution approached, Goldman had longed to join demonstrations for them. She had felt "like a fool" for doing so little in the face of their "impending butchery." When word reached her that the two had been put to death, memories of Haymarket rushed back to her: "I am going through the agonies of forty years ago." There was a difference, however. "Then I had my life before me to take up the cause for those killed. Now I have nothing."

Goldman did have her past. For years her friends had urged her to write her autobiography. In fact, she had been considering such a project since her 1918 jailing. Now she had the time, the need, and the inclination to write. With her movement in total disarray and her finances virtually depleted, she looked upon her memoirs as a potential source of ideological order and hard currency. With her best days behind her, she set out to focus on those forty years, beginning with Haymarket, when all of her adult life lay before her.

With poet Edna St. Vincent Millay as chair, a group of friends collected over $2,500 so that Goldman could spend at least a year rethinking, reliving, and revising her tumultuous life. An additional $3,000 was raised to buy a small cottage in the French fishing village of Saint-Tropez. From her window Goldman could look out across the Mediterranean and think back across her years on the firing line, all without access to her personal papers (which the Department of Justice had confiscated in 1917) and without great confidence in her ability to write. She knew she could move an audience with the spoken word, but would readers pay attention to her?

For what turned out to be better than two years, Goldman hammered away at her typewriter, unable to let go of a single experience, unwilling to believe that her potential reader would be better served by brevity and reflection. Despite fallen arches, swollen veins, poor eyesight, and general fatigue, she stayed with the task. By the end of her labors, it was apparent to her that she had been wrong at least once when she was a young girl. At twenty she claimed that she had rid herself of her "meaningless past," much as one would throw aside a "worn-out garment." In fact, the past was anything but meaningless to Goldman, either at twenty or at sixty. If she had tossed off the "garment" at twenty, she had never been able to throw it away for good. Her past was always with her, whether she chose to wear a piece of it on her sleeve or when the whole garment was stored away in the closets of her mind.

The new Emma Goldman of *Living My Life* was a woman who had warred with her oppressors, whether they were the authority figures in her life or the private devils of depression and jealousy. The new Goldman was not entirely a liberated woman, however. She was just as much a victim as the old Goldman had ever been, whether her adversary was her hateful father or a vengeful President Wilson.

In Goldman's recollection, her happiest years were her middle years, the years between President McKinley's assassination and President Wilson's war. These were the years when the "void" in her life was filled with rapt listeners and with Reitman. There was, of course, a measure of truth in all this, for many happy days were strewn among those sixteen years. But the "void" still remained, as did a gnawing sense that her life had been a series of failed battles.

Another battle remained to be fought. Her initial understanding with her publisher, Alfred A. Knopf, was that Goldman produce a one-volume book, concluding with her deportation from the United States. At the last minute, Knopf asked for a chapter on her two years in Russia. Upset by the request, Goldman churned out 200 pages on her Russian experiences. In response, Knopf insisted that the book now had to be sold in two volumes for not less than $7.50. Goldman was furious. Her potential readers, she thundered, could not afford to pay such an exorbitant price. All her life she had "worked for the mass." Now she wanted that "mass" to be able to read her life story. Five dollars was as much as Knopf should charge.

Library requests, especially in major cities, were brisk, even if sales were not. But Goldman had written her autobiography to make a little money, as well as to exorcise her devils. Here was Knopf, one more greedy capitalist, blocking her road to financial health by selling the book for $7.50 in depression-bound America.

Goldman had one more reason for reliving her life via her pen. It was her last chance to recapture her American past. These were years of struggle and failure, but among them were days of fame and romance. Struggling, and failing, to find either in exile, she set out to restore those days when she was in full possession of both. Anarchists have always been chary about parading their possessions. Not Goldman, who was far from an ordinary anarchist, and whose possessions were not the usual treasures. People and her ideal meant more to her than money and things. In America she could never call Reitman her own, and she was forever unable to realize her ideal.

But there were days—even years—when she could at least dream of embracing both. Now it was time to relive those days and to state her case as an anarchist and an American. At sea for better than a decade, Goldman wanted to give her American readers a chance to recall her years among them. Worried about being lost and forgotten, she hoped that others would see her as she wanted to be seen: a modern Jefferson or Thoreau in the person of a diminutive, but not small-minded, "grandmotherly" radical.

As she entered her seventh decade, Goldman was a woman with few illusions and even fewer dreams. She did dream of being loved again, and she did continue to love her ideal. But she was under no illusion that either was immediately, if ever, realizable. One more dream, however, did remain to her. Having been at odds with America and at sea from it, she dreamed of spending her final years where she had lived the bulk of her life. *Living My Life* was both a testament and a plea: Remember Emma Goldman as an American radical, and permit her to come home again.

CHAPTER TEN

At Home, But Never at Peace

❖
❖

for only 90 days

More than two years passed between the publication of *Living My Life* and Goldman's 1934 return to the United States. By then the political mood in Washington had changed dramatically. During the New Deal of Franklin Roosevelt, ancient memories of Red Emma were fading rapidly. Less an object of fear than of quaint historical interest, the "grandmotherly" Goldman had become more an artifact than a threat. Even conservatives were inclined to forget segments of her past, given her more recent conversion to anti-Sovietism. A "stout, old woman with gray bobbed hair" (in the reportorial eye of the Boston *Herald*) was not about to consort with assassins or lead food riots. She was anxious to return to the scene of her triumphs and failures and to the country she "loved with open eyes."

For ninety days Goldman toured and spoke from New York to St. Louis. Followed by agents of J. Edgar Hoover's Bureau of Investigation and a horde of reporters, she visited sixteen cities. Despite the ban on political lectures, she freely attacked both German fascism and Soviet Communism. In fact, as of 1934, Goldman was relatively rare among those on the left in her judgment that the similarities between fascism and communism far outweighed their differences.

Hoover's agents tried hard to detect sympathy for Communism in Goldman's speeches. None was to be found. Communists and fellow travelers were in her audiences, but they were not there to pay tribute to her. Instead, they heckled her mercilessly. She had "sold out" to the American establishment in order to secure her reentry. She had come back to capitalist America simply to "make cash." She was nothing more than another "reactionary" out to save capitalism from its own follies.

Attacked from the left, Goldman the anarchist could still draw critics from the right. The Hearst press, for example, revived the label "Red Emma" and recalled her years as one of the "leading Communists" in America. In Washington, the Daughters of the American Revolution refused to rent her Constitution Hall. In Columbus, she was unable to speak when World War I veterans threatened to raid the hall.

Despite all this controversy, Goldman's lecture tour was a financial disaster. Hoping to attract huge crowds, she had hired the James Pond Agency to promote her tour. The selection was not a wise one. Pond's clientele ran almost exclusively to theatrical celebrities; hence his decision to rent large halls and charge two dollars a lecture. This was a grand sum to the typical Goldman listener. As a result, Goldman generally appeared before sparse gatherings, made to seem even sparser by the sizes of the spaces Pond had chosen.

Like Alfred Knopf, Pond now felt the heat generated by Goldman's wrath. Angry at being treated like "some circus performer," she decided to take organizational matters into her own hands. Chicago was her last chance to attract a good crowd. At her insistence, the admission price was to be no more than 45 cents. The result was a series of capacity crowds of 2,000 people and more. All along, Pond had argued that Goldman's reputation was to blame for her poor draws. At the end of her tour he was proved wrong. But then, a good number of Chicagoans had always been interested in what Emma Goldman had had to say.

Despite her money troubles, Goldman relished her ninety days so thoroughly that she found it "extremely painful" to leave. She had restored family connections and regained confidence in her ability to speak to American audiences. Besides, she sighed, "real work was impossible in Europe; it is only here that I can find myself."

In her Toronto hotel room, Goldman recorded her "impressions of America." The Americans of 1934, she concluded, "owned their own souls" as the Americans of 1919 had not. There was a "strange" confidence across the face of her "old battlefield," a confidence induced by the presence of Franklin Roosevelt and the "free reign" that he had given to all thoughts and ideas. Judging Roosevelt far superior to his "tenth-rate predecessors," Goldman insisted that she was still a "diehard anarchist." The president may have "awaken[ed] to the fact that government is for the workingman," but the New Deal had still not gone far enough to remove the "injustices of the industrial system." "Rugged individualism" remained the American motto. Sweatshops could still be found in city after city, and tobacco roads continued to crisscross the countryside.

Yet the "rebellious spirit" of labor and youth, as well as the general "cultural freedom unleashed by the New Deal," had convinced Goldman that America was in the midst of a "veritable upheaval." Of course, it was "regrettable" to this confirmed anarchist that American workers had had to wait for a "cue from Washington" before acting to organize their "collective strength." But that signal had at least been given — and taken. Now it was only a matter of time before Roosevelt, or a successor, would "reap the whirlwind."

Just as Goldman had seemed ready to endorse the New Deal, she recovered in time to rediscover her anarchist past. The future, she concluded, rested not with old politicians but with young radicals. Prior to the Great War, the only youthful upstarts in America were "Russian Jewish rebels." To find a "thoughtful American under thirty-five" was akin to coming upon a "pin in a haystack." Now young questioning Americans inhabited every college campus Goldman visited. Although they had "not learned as much in five or six years" as she had taken away from her ten months on Blackwell's Island, she was impressed with their "determination to mold their own lives," as well as gratified by their refusal "to be a party to war at any price." Her own antiwar work "had not been in vain" after all.

Nor had Goldman's work on behalf of the availability of birth control. By 1934, Chicago alone had eight clinics that dispensed contraceptives. "Preachers, rabbis, and ultra-respectable ladies" had come to accept birth control "as a matter of course."

Goldman left the United States as she had come, an anarchist and a radical, but one with little hope for the future of anarchism in the United States. Her American comrades were "as petty and cantankerous as always." They "stick in their own little groups with twenty-five opinions for a dozen people. . . . My faith in anarchism would be shattered indeed if I were to believe that these people will construct a new society. . . . Even if they could, I would be the last one to want to live in it, for it would be more unbearable than now."

Still, Goldman's faith in the *idea* of anarchism had not been destroyed. It continued to "burn like a red, white flame in my soul." When she left the United States against her will for the second time, she left convinced that America was finally "coming of age," that Americans were closer to understanding the meaning of "real liberty and social equity." She also left prepared to die "in exile and poverty," rather than have "anything detract one iota from [the] beauty and logic" of her ideal. Ideas do die hard, but at least Goldman managed to refrain from imposing her version of utopia on anyone else, either because she shied away from ever defining it precisely or because she ultimately distrusted all wielders of power, herself included.

Having been welcomed to America as an exile rather than an anarchist, Goldman returned to Europe with the full knowledge that she was both. When she left for Saint-Tropez, via Canada, she was not resigned to the first designation. One day, she hoped, a U.S. government would bring her home for good. One day her exiled status would be removed by the stroke of a pen. Until then, she would continue to profess her anarchism proudly.

During the two years immediately following her U.S. tour, Goldman became increasingly pessimistic about the willingness of the masses to rally behind her ideal. Events in Europe in the mid-1930s had convinced her that the masses were pawns in the hands of demagogic politicians. Hitler was the main culprit, but he was only one of a number of "unscrupulous spellbinders" who had captured the attention and the loyalty of the masses.

In truth, Goldman had seldom exhibited great confidence in the "visionless" masses. Given their "herdlike idiocy," what was a revolutionary to do? To complicate matters, good anarchists had to answer a new and difficult question as the 1930s unfolded: How should an anarchist respond to fascist governments? More specifically, should an anarchist cooperate with communists and others on the political left who opposed fascism? Goldman drew a line that kept all Stalinists on the other side of her political fence. When antifascists of many varieties were urging "no enemies to the left," Goldman could not agree. Stalinism, to her, was simply another form of fascism, because it was another form of totalitarianism.

After June 1936, Goldman had to make all of her political and personal calculations without Berkman. In poor health for a number of years, he had come to rely on her to be his eyes and ears to events in the larger world, for she had continued to travel and to lecture. By the early spring of 1936, Berkman needed much more than either Goldman or Eckstein could provide. His physical condition and financial situation were deteriorating apace with the collapse of international anarchism. Money had always been a problem for both Berkman and Goldman. Communist propaganda aside, the two did not live luxuriously in exile. Berkman's situation was more precarious, because he had to support two without being able to count on a fairly regular stream of lecture fees. Forced to rely on friends (Goldman included), he was reduced to buying lottery tickets in a futile attempt to escape indebtedness.

Caught between having "not enough to live on and too much to die for" (which was Goldman's characterization of their common situation), Berkman finally decided that he could tolerate the tension no more. Besides, he had increasing doubts that he did have "too much to die for." On a personal level, his triangular relationship with Goldman and Eckstein had grown unbearable. Wildly different in age, temperament, and political philosophy, the two women shared only their affection for Berkman and their jealousy of one another. In late June 1936 he suffered a relapse following two operations for prostate cancer earlier in the year. Having planned a surprise visit to Saint-Tropez to celebrate Goldman's sixty-seventh birthday, he could only send his regrets instead.

The morning after she received his letter, Goldman was awakened by a telephone call from Nice: Berkman was near death, the victim of a botched suicide attempt. As he had failed to kill Henry Clay Frick, so did he manage to bungle his own execution—again. He lived in agony for sixteen hours before succumbing, leaving only a note asking forgiveness from the two women in his life and an estate of eighty dollars.

Nothing in Goldman's crisis-strewn life ever hit her harder than Berkman's death. Nothing could remove its "crushing weight." Pondering her loss left her "absolutely stranded." In fact, the more she thought about his death, the more she questioned the purpose of her own life.

Though Goldman would hardly have agreed, nothing short of an act of providence could have altered her tortured frame of mind. Yet within a matter of weeks something happened that must have seemed providential to even an unbelieving Goldman. On July 19, Spanish workers took up arms against the Spanish military, and civil war in Spain was fully engaged. Within a matter of weeks, so was Goldman.

Disdainful of Spanish males and their exaggerated sense of their own superiority, Goldman held back from immediately committing herself to republican Spain's fight against fascism. In September, however, she received an invitation from Spanish anarchists to come to Barcelona to lend support to them. Their "call," she wrote a friend in early September, "saved my life. . . . It has pulled me out from under the awful pall that was hanging over me."

Here was a chance for true anarchism to take root. Here agricultural and worker cooperatives were springing spontaneously into existence. Here freedom and equality could grow and flourish together. How could Goldman say no? She was sixty-seven, but age mattered little to someone who always thought her "life should end as it began, fighting." Never mind the prospect of having to work with those notorious Spanish males. The future of anarchism was at stake.

When Goldman entered Barcelona in early October, she found herself in an anarchist-controlled city for the first time in her life. At a mass rally thousands turned out to hear her call for Barcelona to become a "shining example" to the rest of the world. "Walking on air," she could barely contain her euphoria. Spain in 1936 was everything that Russia in 1920 had proved not to be. There was no Spanish Lenin controlling the course of the revolution from on high. Instead, intelligent committed Spanish workers and peasants seemed to be in charge of their own revolution.

Before the year was out, however, Goldman had left Spain and the Soviets had arrived. While her departure was brief, theirs was not; and therein lies her story of the "assassination of the Spanish Revolution" and of perhaps the greatest disappointment of her public life. In mid-November the embattled Spanish anarchists had asked Goldman to go to London to recruit financial and political support. She still hated London, and she especially resented the prospect of living there when she could be in the midst of an anarchist revolution somewhere else. The battle was being waged in Spain, not in England; and Goldman no doubt sensed that this was her last chance to be at the center of the fight. With great reluctance, she agreed to go.

Arriving in London in late December, Goldman feared that the tide of battle had already turned against anarchism in Spain. She also thought that there was little she could do—in Spain or in England—to restore the initiative to her Spanish allies. No doubt the Spanish anarchists knew as much themselves when they accepted military support from the Soviet Union.

From London, Goldman complained repeatedly of the communist "sabotage" of the anarchists' revolution. It did no good. Nor did return trips to Barcelona in September and

October 1937 and in August 1938. The situation was beyond anything that any single individual could reverse. She flailed away at the communists, the fascists, and the "so-called Western democracies"—all were "in league to crush the Spanish people," and none was ready to permit "so great a libertarian experiment to continue."

Goldman left Spain for the last time in December 1938, downcast but not defeated. Spain at least had given the world a glimpse of what might have been, but for the intervention of the twin evils of communism and fascism. The people of Barcelona had tried to build a society minus the greed of capitalism and the terror of communism. This was her vision of the anarchist middle way. That her ideal had been crushed in Spain could never convince Goldman that it could not be resurrected another day and in another place.

Goldman had been many things in her life, but she was never a fatalist, until another European war approached in 1939. Nor had she ever been a pacifist. Still, she was unwilling to endorse a war against Hitler, even as he waged a proxy war in Spain and moved brazenly to acquire Austria and Czechoslovakia. Her anger at the failure of the so-called democracies to support Spanish workers and peasants in their fight against fascism dictated her refusal to choose between Hitler and his targets. Yet she found it much harder to hold to an antiwar position in 1939 than she had at any point between 1914 and 1917. She was, after all, a convinced antifascist. And German-Jewish anarchists, whether escapees from Nazi Germany or not, invariably supported a war against Hitler.

When Hitler and Stalin entered into their Nazi-Soviet Pact in late August 1939, Goldman was not surprised. She had been predicting as much for at least six years. Letter after letter from her overworked typewriter was filled with smug I-told-you-sos in the weeks following the treaty. Moreover, without formal knowledge of the pact's full contents, she correctly predicted that Stalin would move to acquire the Baltic provinces. "Mark my word . . . such brazen fraud and open pilfering the world has never seen." Still, this alliance of the

two regimes she detested beyond all others was not enough
to bring her to support a war against them. Hitler, she contended through the fall and winter of 1939–1940, must be
defeated "by the German people themselves."

Having disengaged from Spain a year earlier, Goldman remained almost silent while Hitler's military machine rolled
across Poland and Stalin's Red Army struggled to gobble up
Finland. She did deliver an occasional blast at the Nazi-Soviet
Pact and at "fellow travelers" who tried to justify Stalin's behavior. "Like worms, they are squirming out of their former
position . . . they are really sickening in their attempt
to . . . turn Stalin's betrayal into the last word of political
acumen."

Could the United States stay out of this war? Goldman
doubted that President Roosevelt had the "stamina to hold out
against Wall Street and the military clique that wants war for
the sake of war." She also knew that this was not quite 1917
all over again. In 1917, Woodrow Wilson needed his comeup-
pance, and Goldman was in robust middle age. In 1939, Hitler
and Stalin deserved to be throttled, and Goldman was a worn
out seventy. Therefore, she chose not to fight very hard against
those who wanted America to fight.

As an anarchist in good standing, Goldman stood back and
declared a plague on many houses. "Stalin's lust for imperial
power is as insatiable as Hitler's. . . . The Western powers have
much to account for before the world. . . . Hitler was made
by the spineless tactics of the democracies."

There were rumors that the Roosevelt administration had
offered to permit Goldman to return to the United States
provided she would attack the communists and work with congressional committees investigating them. Preferring continued
exile to becoming a "tool [of] reactionaries," Goldman let it be
known that she would decline any such deal. Coming home
was not *that* important to a woman who had been the subject
of more than her share of official investigations. Better to sit
and stew in France than to do the bidding of Washington. Having been a "prisoner in America" following the loss of her claim
to citizenship, she was not about to become the prisoner of

a U.S. government, even if the price of her treasured freedom was her continuing exile. Principles had always been more important to her than personal contentment. On that score she could be infuriating to her friends and enemies, as well as occasionally hard on herself.

A single woman almost all her days, Goldman was as independent a woman at seventy as she had been at sixteen. That sense of independence had led her to fight her own battles, whether political or psychological. At times she could be exhilarated by the possibilities of her ideal. At other times she was singed by one or the other of her "two fires." Many times she was burdened by disappointments and beset by doubts. But always she faced life with a sense of self-reliance to match the sturdiest of mythical American Jeffersonians.

During the winter of 1939–1940, Goldman's combined faith in herself and her ideal was put to its severest test. Anarchism had collapsed in Spain, Hitler and Stalin were astride Europe, and the mass of men and women continued to live lives of quiet submission. At least she would not surrender, not to cynical Washington-inspired deals, not to her own bouts with depression, and not to a future without her ideal. In the meantime, she would wait. Maybe someday she could come home on her own terms. Maybe someday the world would turn to her ideal. Maybe someday another platform and another audience would be waiting for her. Goldman may have been seventy, but resignation was never her intention, or her frame of mind.

Epilogue

In the late fall of 1939, Goldman learned of the plight of four young Italian anarchists who were scheduled for deportation by the Canadian government. With the Sacco-Vanzetti case still very much on her mind, with the memory of her own forced exile always fresh, and in memory of Berkman, she went to work to raise money for one of the four, Arturo Bartolotti, who had been jailed for possessing a revolver at the time of his arrest. Acting as if nothing else in the world was as important as the fate of "A.B." (another Alexander Berkman?), Goldman sailed for Canada to organize a "Save Arturo Bartolotti Committee." The campaign, which lasted through the winter, ended successfully with Bartolotti's release.

Goldman could not have been more pleased had she defeated Hitler and Stalin with a single blow. But her happiness was short-lived. Within days of her victory she suffered a massive stroke while still in Toronto. Ironically, Bartolotti was just then gathering a number of friends to spend the evening celebrating with Goldman when he learned of her condition.

Recuperation was slow and arduous. Completely paralyzed on her right side, Goldman could speak only a few words—and those with great difficulty. Now it was again her turn to have a committee formed to raise money on her behalf. Organized by Roger Baldwin among others, the Friends of Emma Goldman swung into action. This time the issue was not her memoirs, let alone bail money following yet another arrest. At this moment literature and politics were suddenly beside the point.

Despite the committee's best efforts, Goldman died on May 14, 1940. In death, she was granted the one wish that had been denied her for nearly twenty-one years: permission to cross the U.S. border for good. She had been a demanding woman all her life. Many times she had been a disappointed woman as well, whether by her own failures or by the failures of others to live up to her expectations. But one of her last petitions was honored after her death. Upon her instructions, Goldman was buried near her Haymarket martyrs in Waldheim Cemetery in Chicago. The request was entirely appropriate. After all, it was their execution that had inspired a young Emma Goldman to commit her own life to anarchism. Now, having lived her life, having kept her faith, she would at last be at rest among friends. Emma Goldman had come home to stay.

A Note on the Sources

❖
❖

This is neither the first nor will it be the last biography of Emma Goldman. Excellent, if very different, biographies have preceded this one. I have benefited from careful readings of Richard Drinnon's *Rebel in Paradise* (Chicago: University of Chicago Press, 1961); Alice Wexler's *Emma Goldman: An Intimate Life* (New York: Pantheon Books, 1984) and *Emma Goldman in Exile* (Boston: Beacon Press, 1989); and Candace Falk's *Love, Anarchy, and Emma Goldman* (New York: Holt, Rinehart, 1984)

Two novels based on Goldman's life have also proved helpful. They are Ethel Mannin's *Red Rose* (London: Jarrolds) and Hutchins Hapgood's *An Anarchist Woman* (New York: Random House, 1909). Although not concerned directly with Goldman's life, N. G. Chernyshevsky's *What Is to Be Done?* (New York: Random House, 1961) ought to be read because of the impact the novel had on Goldman's life.

Shorter pieces concerning aspects of Goldman's life include essays by Blanche Wiesen Cook, "Female Support Networks and Political Activism: Lillian Wald, Crystal Eastman, and Emma Goldman," in *A Heritage of Her Own,* edited by Nancy Cott and Elizabeth Pleck (New York: Simon and Schuster, 1979); Harold Goldberg, "Goldman and Berkman View the Bolshevik Regime," in *Slavonic and East European Review* 34 (April 1975), pp. 272–276; Hutchins Hapgood, "Emma Goldman's Anarchism," in *The Bookman* (February 1911); Hipployte

Havel's introduction to *Anarchism and Other Essays;* Freda Kirchwey, "Emma Goldman," in *The Nation*, December 2, 1931; H. L. Mencken's "Two Views of Russia," in *American Mercury* (May 1924); Henry Pachter, "The Private Lives of Rebels," in *Harper's Magazine* (August 1975); Alix Shulman, "Dancing in the Revolution: Emma Goldman's Feminism" in *Socialist Review* (March–April 1982); Ordway Tead, "Emma Goldman Speaks," in *Yale Review* (June 1932); Alice Wexler, "The Early Life of Emma Goldman," in *The Psychohistorical Review* 8 (Spring 1980), pp. 7–21. Floyd Dell's *Women as World Builders: Studies in Modern Feminism* (Chicago: Forbes, 1913) contains an essay on Goldman.

Primary sources consulted include the Emma Goldman collection at the Tamiment Library of New York University, which includes correspondence from her years in exile, as well as material relating to her 1917 trial; the Goldman collection of the New York Public Library, which also deals with her life after 1919; the Mugar Memorial Library of Boston University, which contains correspondence between Goldman and Almeda Sperry, as well as between Goldman and Ben Reitman; Yale University, which houses the Harry Weinberger collection; and the University of Illinois, which contains the Ben Reitman papers.

Works by Goldman herself have been invaluable. They include her autobiography, *Living My Life* (New York: Knopf, 1931). Goldman did not always tell her story accurately or well, but she did tell it at great length and with great passion. If used carefully, it can inform and instruct any student of Goldman's life. The volumes of *Mother Earth* (1906–1917), which she edited at various times during those eleven years and for which she often wrote, contain much information on the state of American anarchism and American radicalism generally. Many of Goldman's essays were originally published in these pages. A record of her speaking tours, as well as a history of what happened on them, can be unearthed from *Mother Earth*. Concerning her 1917 trial for obstructing the draft, Mother Earth Publishing Association published "Anarchism on Trial: The Speeches of Alexander Berkman and Emma Goldman Before

the U.S. District Court in the City of New York, July, 1917."
A good number of her most provocative essays can be found
in her *Anarchism and Other Essays* (Port Washington: Kennikat
Press, 1969) and in *Red Emma Speaks: Selected Writings and
Speeches by Emma Goldman,* edited by Alix Shulman (New York:
Random House, 1972). Her sometimes frank and always passionate correspondence with Alexander Berkman has been
published in *Nowhere at Home: Letters From Exile of Emma Goldman and Alexander Berkman,* edited by Richard and Anna Maria
Drinnon (New York: Schocken Books, 1975). There are two
volumes on her two years in the Soviet Union: *My Disillusionment in Russia* (1922) and *My Further Disillusionment in Russia*
(1924). She also wrote a biography of sister anarchist, Voltaraine de Cleyre, titled simply *Voltaraine de Cleyre* (Berkeley
Heights: Oriole Press, 1932) and *The Social Significance of the
Modern Drama* (Boston: Richard G. Badger, 1914). Other Goldman essays include "What I Believe," *New York World* (July 19,
1908); "Bolsheviks Shooting Anarchists," *Freedom* (January
1922); "Persecution of Russian Anarchists," *Freedom* (August
1922); "The Bolshevik Government and the Anarchists," *Freedom* (October 1922); "Women of the Russian Revolution," *Time
and Tide* (May 8, 1925); "Johann Most," *American Mercury* (June
1926); "Reflections on the General Strike,"*Freedom* (August–September 1926); "The Voyage of the *Buford*," *American
Mercury* (September 1931); "The Assassination of McKinley,"
American Mercury (September 1931); "The Tragedy of the Political Exiles," *The Nation* (October 10, 1934); "Was My Life
Worth Living?" *Harper's Monthly Magazine* (December 1934);
"There Is No Communism in Russia," *American Mercury* (April
1935); "Anarchists and Elections," *Vanguard* (August–September 1936); "Berkman's Last Days," *Vanguard* (August–September 1936); "The Soviet Executions," *Vanguard* (October–November 1936).

Autobiographies of Goldman allies or contemporaries include Jane Addams, *Twenty Years at Hull House* (New York:
Macmillan, 1911); Margaret Anderson, *My Thirty Years War*
(London: Knopf, 1930); Sherwood Anderson, *Sherwood Anderson's Memoirs* (New York: Harcourt Brace, 1942); Angelica

Balabanoff, *My Life* (New York: Harpers, 1938); Alexander Berkman, *Prison Memoirs of an Anarchist* (New York: Mother Earth Publishing Association, 1912); Floyd Dell, *Homecoming: An Autobiography* (Port Washington: Kennikat Press, 1969); Isadora Duncan, *My Life* (New York: Boni and Liveright, 1927); Max Eastman, *Enjoyment of Living* (New York: Harpers, 1948); Eastman, *Love and Revolution* (New York: Random House, 1964); Elizabeth Gurley Flynn, *The Rebel Girl* (New York: International Publishers, 1976); Joseph Freeman, *An American Testament* (London: Victor Gollancz, 1938); Frederick Howe, *Confessions of a Reformer* (New York: Scribner's, 1925); Hutchins Hapgood, *A Victorian in the Modern World* (New York: Harcourt Brace, 1939); Alexandra Kollontai, *The Autobiography of a Sexually Emancipated Communist Woman* (New York: Schocken Books, 1975); Peter Kropotkin, *Memoirs of a Revolutionist* (Boston, 1899); Isaac Don Levine, *Eyewitness to History* (New York: Hawthorne, 1973); Mabel Dodge Luhan, *Intimate Memories* (New York: Harcourt Brace, 1936); Henry Miller, *My Life and Times* (La Jolla, California: Gemini Smith, 1975); Kate Richard O'Hare, *In Prison* (Seattle: University of Washington Press, 1976); Bertrand Russell *Autobiography of Bertrand Russell* (Boston: Little, Brown and Company, 1968); Margaret Sanger, *An Autobiography* (New York: Dover, 1971); Upton Sinclair, *American Outpost: A Book of Reminiscences* (New York: Farrar and Rinehart, 1932); Lincoln Steffens, *The Autobiography of Lincoln Steffens* (New York: Harcourt Brace, 1931); Bertram Wolfe, *A Life in Two Centuries* (New York: Stein and Day, 1980).

General works on the subject of anarchism include Paul Avrich, *Anarchist Portraits* (Princeton: Princeton University Press, 1988); *The Anarchists in the Russian Revolution* (Ithaca: Cornell University Press, 1973); *The Russian Anarchists* (Princeton: Princeton University Press, 1967); Alexander Berkman, *Now and After: The ABC of Communist Anarchism* (New York: Vanguard Press, 1929); April Carter, *The Political Theory of Anarchism* (New York: Harper and Row, 1971); David DeLeon, *The American as Anarchist* (Baltimore: Johns Hopkins University Press, 1978); James Joll, *The Anarchists* (London: Eyre and Spottiswoode, 1964); Dyer Lum, *The Economics of Anarchy* (New

York: Twentieth Century Publishing Company, 1890); James Martin, *Men Against the State: The Expositors of Individualist Anarchists in America, 1827–1908* (Colorado Springs: Ralph Myles, 1970); William Nowlin, "The Political Thought of Alexander Berkman," Ph.D. dissertation, Tufts University, 1980; Terry Perlin, "Anarchist-Communism in America, 1890–1914," Ph.D. dissertation, Brandeis University, 1970; William Reichert, *Partisans of Freedom: A Study of American Anarchism* (Bowling Green University Press, 1976); Rudolf Rocker *Anarchism and Anarcho-Syndicalism* (London: Freedom Press, 1973); Henry Silverman (ed.), *American Radical Thought: The Libertarian Tradition* (Lexington, Massachusetts: D.C. Heath, 1970); Laurence Veysey, *The Communal Experience: Anarchist and Mystical Countercultures in America* (New York: Harper and Row, 1973); Sidney Warren, *American Freethought, 1860–1914* (New York: Columbia University Press, 1943); George Woodcock, *Anarchism: A History of Libertarian Ideas and Movements* (New York: World Publishing, 1962).

Articles include Paul Avrich, "Kropotkin in America," *International Review of Social History* (1980); Alexander Berkman, "The Anarchist Movement Today," *Freedom* (February 1934); Hyman Berman, "A Cursory View of the Jews and Labor Movement: An Historical Survey," *American Jewish Historical Quarterly* (December 1962); H. M. Douty, "The Word and the Deed: Anarchism Revisited," *Monthly Labor Review* (January 1966); Sidney Fine, "Anarchism and the Assassination of McKinley," *American Historical Review* (1955); Walter Laquer, "Visionaries," *Atlas* (January 1965); Bernard Lewis, "The Assassins: An Historical Essay," *Encounter* (November 1967); Charles Madison, "Anarchism in the United States," *Journal of the History of Ideas* (January 1945); Blaine McKinley, "Anarchist Jeremiads: American Anarchists and American History," *Journal of American Culture* (Summer 1983); McKinley, " 'A Religion of the New Time': Anarchist Memorials to the Haymarket Martyrs, 1888–1917," *Labor History* (Summer 1987); McKinley, " 'The Quagmire of Necessity': American Anarchists and the Dilemmas of Vocation," *American Quarterly* (Winter 1982); D. Novak, "Place of Anarchism in Political Thought," *Review of*

Politics (June 1958); Susan Poirier, "Emma Goldman, Ben Reitman, and Reitman's Wives: A Study in Relationships," *Women's Studies* (February 1988); William Reichert, "Toward a New Understanding of Anarchism," *Western Political Quarterly* (December 1967); Michael Weszin, "Albert J. Nock and the Anarchist Elitist Tradition in America," *American Quarterly* (Summer 1961); Victor Yarros, "Philosophical Anarchism: Its Rise, Decline and Eclipse," *American Journal of Sociology* (January 1936).

General studies and monographs concerning women's history as it relates to the life and career of Emma Goldman include Mary Jo Buhle, *Women and American Socialism, 1870–1920* (Urbana: University of Illinois Press, 1981); Nancy Cott, *The Grounding of Modern Feminism* (New Haven: Yale University Press, 1987); Carl Degler, *At Odds* (New York: Oxford University Press, 1980); Barbara Epstein, *The Politics of Domesticity* (Middletown, Connecticut: Wesleyan University Press, 1981); Sara Evans, *Born for Liberty* (New York: The Free Press, 1989); Eleanor Flexner, *Century of Struggle* (Harvard University Press, 1959); Estelle Freedman, *Their Sisters Keepers: Women's Prison Reform in America 1830–1930* (Ann Arbor: University of Michigan Press, 1981); Linda Gordon, *Women's Bodies, Women's Right: A Social History of Birth Control in America* (New York: Penguin Books, 1977); Mary Hill, *Charlotte Perkins Gilman: The Making of a Radical Feminist* (Philadelphia: Temple University Press, 1980); David Kennedy, *Birth Control in America: The Career of Margaret Sanger* (New Haven: Yale University Press, 1970); Alice Kessler-Harris, *Out to Work* (New York: Oxford University Press, 1982); Aileen Kraditor, *The Ideas of the Women's Suffrage Movement, 1880–1920* (New York: Columbia University Press, 1965); Margaret Marsh, *Anarchist Women, 1870–1920* (Philadelphia: Temple University Press, 1981); William O'Neill, *Everyone Was Brave* (Chicago: Quadrangle Books, 1969); Philip Foner, *Kate Richards O'Hare: Selected Writings and Speeches* (Baton Rouge: Louisiana State University Press, 1982); Ruth Rosen, *The Lost Sisterhood* (Baltimore: Johns Hopkins University Press, 1982); June Sochen, *Consecrate Every Day: The Public Lives of Jewish Women, 1880–1980* (Albany: State University of New York Press, 1981); June Sochen, *Movers and Shakers:*

American Women Thinkers and Activists, 1900–1970 (New York: Quadrangle, 1973); Lynn Weiner, *From Working Girl to Working Mother: The Female Labor Force in the United States, 1820–1980* (Chapel Hill: University of North Carolina Press, 1985).

Biographies of significant Goldman contemporaries include Sara Alpern, *Freda Kirchwey: A Woman of the Nation* (Cambridge: Harvard University Press, 1987); Paul Avrich, *An American Anarchist: The Life of Voltairine de Cleyre* (Princeton: Princeton University Press, 1978); Roger Bruns, *The Damndest Radical: The Life and Work of Ben Reitman* (Urbana: University of Illinois Press, 1987); Bruce Clayton, *Forgotten Prophet: The Life of Randolph Bourne* (Baton Rouge: Louisiana State University Press, 1984); Joseph Conlin, *Big Bill Haywood and the Radical Union Movement* Syracuse University Press, 1969); Blanche Wiesen Cook, *Crystal Eastman: On Women and Revolution* (New York: Oxford University Press, 1978); Bernard Crick, *George Orwell* (London: Secker and Warburg, 1980); Barbara Gelb, *So Short a Time: A Biography of John Reed and Louise Bryant* (New York: Norton, 1973); Ray Ginger, *The Bending Cross* (New York: Collier Books, 1966); Justin Kaplan, *Lincoln Steffens: A Biography* (New York: Simon and Schuster, 1974); Peggy Lawson, *Roger Baldwin* (Boston: Houghton Mifflin, 1976); Robert Rosenstone, *Romantic Revolutionary: A Life of John Reed* (New York: Knopf, 1975); William O'Neill, *The Last Romantic: A Life of Max Eastman* (New York: Oxford University Press, 1978); Nick Salvatore, *Eugene Debs: Citizen and Socialist* (Urbana: University of Illinois Press, 1983); George Woodcock and Ivan Avakumovic, *The Anarchist Prince: A Biographical Study of Peter Kropotkin* (London: T.V. Boardman and Co., 1950).

General monographs that relate to the life and career of Emma Goldman include Daniel Aaron, *Writers on the Left* (New York: Harcourt Brace, 1961); Paul Avrich, *The Haymarket Tragedy* (Princeton: Princeton University Press, 1986); Paul Avrich, *The Kronstadt Rebellion* (Princeton: Princeton University Press, 1970); Murray Bookchin, *The Spanish Anarchists: The Heroic Years, 1868–1936* (New York: Harper and Row, 1977); Franz Borkenau, *The Spanish Cockpit* (Ann Arbor: University of Michigan Press, 1971); Gerald Brenan, *The Spanish Labyrinth* (Cambridge: Cambridge University Press, 1969); Van Wyck

Brooks, *The Confident Years: 1885–1915* (New York: E. P. Dutton, 1952); E. Malcolm Carroll, *Soviet Communism and Western Opinion, 1919–1921* (Chapel Hill: University of North Carolina Press, 1965); David Caute, *The Fellow Travelers* (London: Weidenfeld and Nicolson, 1973); William Henry Chamberlin, *The Russian Revolution, 1917–1921* (New York: Macmillan, 1935); Peter Cohn, *The Divided Mind: Ideology and Imagination in America, 1898–1917* (Cambridge: Cambridge University Press, 1983); Joseph Conlin, *Bread and Roses Too: Studies of the Wobblies* (Westport, Connecticut: Greenwood Press, 1969); Robert Daniels, *The Conscience of the Revolution* (Cambridge, Massachusetts: Harvard University Press, 1960); Isaac Deutscher, *The Prophet Armed* (New York: Vintage, 1965); Richard Drinnon, *The Blast: An Introduction and an Appraisal* (Lewisburg, Pennsylvania: Bucknell University Press, 1970); Melvyn Dubofsky, *Industrialism and the American Worker, 1865–1920* (Arlington Heights, Illinois: Harlan Davidson, 1985); Melvyn Dubofsky, *We Shall Be All: A History of the Industrial Workers of the World* (Chicago: Quadrangle Books, 1969); Lewis Erenberg, *Steppin' Out: New York Nightlife and the Transformation of American Culture, 1890–1930* (Chicago: University of Chicago Press, 1981); Peter Filene, *Americans and the Soviet Experiment, 1917–1933* (Cambridge, Massachusetts: Harvard University Press, 1967); Leslie Fishbein, *Rebels in Bohemia: The Radicals of the Masses, 1911–1917* (Chapel Hill: University of North Carolina Press, 1981); William Fishman, *Jewish Radicals: From Czarist State to London Ghetto* (New York: Pantheon, 1974); Richard Frost, *The Mooney Case* (Palo Alto, California: Stanford University Press, 1968); Herbert Gutman, *Work, Culture and Society in Industrializing America* (New York: Knopf, 1976); Oscar Handlin, *The Uprooted* (Boston: Little, Brown, 1951); Samuel Hays, *The Response to Industrialism, 1885–1914* (Chicago: University of Chicago Press, 1959); John Higham, *Strangers in the Land* (New York: Atheneum, 1965); Irving Howe, *World of Our Fathers* (New York: Harcourt Brace Jovanovich, 1976); Gabriel Jackson, *The Spanish Republicans and the Civil War* (Princeton: Princeton University Press, 1965); Donald Johnson, *The Challenge to American Freedoms: World War I and the Rise of the ACLU* (Lexington, Kentucky: University of Kentucky Press, 1963); Harvey Klehr,

The Heyday of American Communism (New York: Basic Books, 1984); Gabriel Kolko, *The Triumph of Conservatism* (New York: Macmillan, 1963); Alan Kraut, *The Huddled Masses: The Immigrant in American Society, 1880–1921* (Arlington Heights, Illinois: Harlan Davidson, 1982); Douglas Little, *Malevolent Neutrality: The United States, Great Britain, and the Origins of the Spanish Civil War* (Ithaca: Cornell University Press, 1985); Christopher Lasch, *The New Radicalism in America, 1889–1963* (New York: Random House, 1965); Henry May, *The End of American Innocence* (New York: Knopf, 1959); Milton Meltzer, *Bread—and Roses: The Struggle of American Labor, 1865–1915* (New York: Knopf, 1967); Sally Miller, *The Radical Immigrant* (New York: Twayne, 1972); Paul Murphy, *World War I and the Origin of Civil Liberties in the United States* (New York: Norton, 1979); Peter Nettl, *Rosa Luxenburg* (New York: Oxford University Press, 1969); George Orwell, *Homage to Catalonia* (New York: Harcourt Brace and World, 1952); H. C. Peterson and Gilbert Fite, *Opponents of War, 1917–1918* (Madison: University of Wisconsin Press, 1957); Richard Polenberg, *Fighting Faiths: The Abrams Case, the Supreme Court, and Free Speech* (New York: Viking, 1987); Louis Post, *The Deportations Delirium of Nineteen-Twenty* (Chicago: Charles Kerr, 1923); Richard Gid Powers, *Secrecy and Power: The Life of J. Edgar Hoover* (New York: The Free Press, 1987); Paul Preston, *The Spanish Civil War, 1936–1939* (London: Weidenfeld and Nicolson, 1986); William Preston, *Aliens and Dissenters: Federal Suppression of Radicals, 1903–1933* (New York: Harper and Row, 1963); Francis Russell, *Sacco and Vanzetti: The Case Resolved* (New York: Harper and Row, 1986); Hal Sears, *The Sex Radicals: Free Love in High Victorian America* (Lawrence: The Regents Press of Kansas, 1977); S. A. Smith, *Red Petrograd* (Cambridge: Cambridge University Press, 1983); Estelle Jelinek, ed., *Women's Autobiography: Essays in Criticism* (Bloomington: Indiana University Press, 1980); Hugh Thomas, *The Spanish Civil War* (New York: Harpers, 1961); Franco Venturi, *Roots of Revolution* (New York: Grosset and Dunlap, 1966); Robert Wiebe, *The Search for Order* (New York: Hill and Wang, 1967); Stephen White, *Britain and the Bolshevik Revolution* (London: Macmillan, 1979).

Index